A Banner To The Nations

By the Same Author

Words From The Scroll Of Fire (Jerusalem 1994)
The Cross Became a Sword, *The Soldiers Of Christ And The First Crusade* (London,1995)
Roots and Branches (ed and cont London, 1998)
Father, Forgive Us: *A Christian Response to the Church's Heritage of Jewish Persecution* (London 2002)
Within the Pale (Solihull, 2004)
Israel: His People, His Land, His Story (ed and cont London 2005)
Ethical Vectors of Warfare, (London 2019)
Aliyah Holy to the Lord (London 2019)
The Dark legacy of Martin Luther (2018)
Eschatology origins and Consequences(due 2018)

By Patricia Frame

Intercession and Aliyah (Carlisle 2012)

A Banner To The Nations

Fred'k Wright
With
Patricia Frame

KDF Chesed Publishing
Colchester, UK

Copyright Fred'k Wright
The right of Fred'k Wright
to be identified as the author of this work
has been asserted by him in accordance
with the Copyright, Designs
and Patents Act 1988

First published 2019

Published by
Chesed Publishing
Colchester

ISBN 978-0-244-50020-7

All rights reserved.
No part of this publication may be reproduced or
transmitted in any form or by any means, electronic,
or mechanical, including photocopy, recording, or
any information storage and retrieval system, without
permission in writing from the publisher

CONTENTS

Acknowledgements 7
Introduction 9
Historical Background 11
Historical Considerations 17
Christian Awakening 25
Boots on the Ground 35
Ethiopia 45
Siberia – Four Corners 57
Belarus 65
The Work Begins in the fSU 71
Indigenous Workers 89
Family Matters 97
CSA Ministries 119
Hindrances and Objections to CSA 139
The Evangelism of Silence and Grace 145
The Changing Face of Aliyah 149
The Rise of Vladimir Putin 159
Those Who Cannot Make Aliyah 165
Afterword 173
Appendix 1 175
Appendix 2 177

Acknowledgements

As the narrator I would like to express my appreciation to those who have helped in the preparation of this work. Thanks firstly to my friend and colleague of over twenty years, Pat Frame, for helping collect testimonies, swapping anecdotes and all of the hard work on the field. Thanks also to Peter Styles for his encouragement and comments. Special thanks to my wife Maria for helping both in the preparation of the text and sharing adventures on the field. Thanks to Charles Gardner for a final edit and John Chamberlain Butt for the tech end of the preparation

Finally, to all those who shared adventures in *aliyah* with us over the past thirty years in diverse countries across the world, often at great personal cost: *Baruch Ha Shem!*

This book is dedicated to those who have served, those who serve and those who will!

Introduction

The year 2019 marked the thirtieth anniversary of the collapse of the mighty Soviet Union and its satellites. These years later we may have thought that the memory is dimming of the great monolithic structure that was the USSR and the iron grip that it kept on its inhabitants, controlling every measure of daily life. In addition, the so-called 'Cold War' had the world in a state of tension anticipating a nuclear conflagration. At the time of writing it appears that Vladimir Putin has effectively re-launched the idea of a mighty Russian empire, commencing with the annexation of the Crimea and Eastern Ukraine along with threats to Poland and the Baltics.

Little did I think that I would be putting the final portions of the work together in the midst of shelling in the Donbas region of Ukraine or that there would be an eruption of violent anti-Semitism in mainland Europe. In one sense this makes the timing of this piece of work even more important.

It was from the initial collapse point of the USSR that the return of the Jewish people in large numbers to their ancient, God-given homeland became not only a possibility but a reality. It seems appropriate, therefore, especially as the majority of the founders of the Christian-sponsored aliyah initiatives are with the Lord, to record some of the events, trials, tribulations and humorous elements of the last thirty-three years. In addition, there are included memories of what we have termed the proto-aliyah movement that undertook the establishment of the biblical basis for the work, along with the prayer initiatives and the building of practical foundations. The first section deals with the historical background from the Jewish point of view through the long and convoluted path that led towards the Christian realisation of the biblical basis and the theological shift towards an understanding of God's plan for His people and their relationship to the land.

The second section looks back to the experiences of those who worked on the field, often in extreme circumstances. Civil wars, shortages of every description, mountains of red tape and officialdom, not to mention the continual problems caused by the weather and primitive conditions became part of everyday life.

The third section looks at how the aliyah process would not be complete without the ministries within the land who help the olim 'settle in', covering everything from legal and administrative problems though to personal, financial and healthcare. It could be said that all needs are met, from those still in the womb to those at the end of their days.

The fourth section considers the changing face of aliyah and the strands of continuity and change.

The final thoughts consider aliyah from the biblical record of the Lord's point of view.

As any work of this nature will never be, so to speak, 'up to date,' the intention has been to celebrate the Lord's goodness and mercy through thirty years of Christian-sponsored aliyah and provide a memoir to encourage future work. It might well be that the days we are living in are those that we thought were far away, or in the pulse of the dream where aliyah may become the prophesied exodus, namely, the death throes of the diaspora and birth pains of the remnant church.

Frederick Wright,
Donbas, March 2019

Chapter 1

Historical Background

Scripture illustrates clearly that God has an ongoing plan for Israel and he is committed to her by everlasting covenant. His never-ending fatherly love and care for Israel is a sign of his faithfulness and holiness, not only toward Israel but as a visual display to all of the nations of his character.

When God called Abram forth to journey to a land he knew not, he told him that he would show him a new land which would be his possession. The Lord swore by his own name that this would be so (Hebrews 6:13).

The Psalmist expresses the matter clearly in Psalm 105:8-11, emphasising continuity through following generations.

He remembers his covenant forever, the promise he made, for a thousand generations. The covenant he made with Abraham, the oath he swore to Isaac, He confirmed it to Jacob as a decree, to Israel as an everlasting covenant: To you I will give the land of Canaan as the portion you will inherit (Genesis 12:7, 17:8, 26:3-4 and Genesis 13-14).

When the people of Israel entered the Promised Land under Joshua's leadership, they were told to destroy the heathens who had previously lived there and be separated (holy) unto God. Since they failed to do this and, from the latter days of Solomon, began to follow the false gods of other peoples, Israel was taken into captivity in Assyria in 729-719 BCE (Before the Christian Era) followed by Judea to Babylon in 605-586 BCE.

In fulfilment of a prophecy delivered by Jeremiah (25:11), the southern tribes of Benjamin and Judah, along with some priests and Levites, returned after 70 years in exile. The events of this minor return are recorded in the books of Ezra and Nehemiah.

Following their failure to recognise Yeshua as Messiah, they were once again dispersed after the fall of Jerusalem in 70 CE and the failure of the Second Revolt in 132-35 – on this occasion for almost 2,000 years and were spread throughout the whole world (the *diaspora*).

God had promised that this dispersion would finally end prior to the return of the Messiah. This return forms the burden of the major prophets, in concert with other Scriptures, ranging from Leviticus through to Malachi. There are at least 141 prophecies concerning the final, irreversible restoration of both the land of Israel, and the chosen people to the land, with Jerusalem, God's chosen city where His presence would dwell, as its eternal capital. Compare, for instance, *Jeremiah 33:11*, which predicts the restoration of both the land and the people, with *Isaiah 43:5-6 "...from the ends of the earth"*.

Ezekiel 36:16-28 predicts that when the people of Israel are restored to their land they will also be restored spiritually:

I will sprinkle clean water on you and you will be clean; I will cleanse you from all your impurities...I will give you a new heart and put a new spirit in you ...you will be my people and I will be your God (*cf* Deut 30:1-6 where Moses predicts this dispersion and restoration (*et al*, Zec 10:8-10. Is 62:1-5).

The people are married to the land. Israel 'the people' and Israel 'the Land' belong together. The exile of the Jewish people profaned God's Name (Ezek *36:20)* and for the sake of His Holy Name, God causes their return (Ezek 36:22). In the body of Scripture, names are not voice labels. Rather, they are descriptions of a person's character. God is concerned for His reputation, which is restored when the people return.

Modern Replacement Theology, now more generally referred to as supercessionism, declares that God broke His relationship with Israel after the Jewish people refused to accept Jesus as their Messiah. The Church became 'Spiritual Israel' to the exclusion of the natural people. Such views are not only unbiblical in the extreme, but also ignore history. The views are also post-biblical in the sense that those holding them do not believe God's word is unchanging and that He is capable of fulfilling it!

Paul explains in Romans 9-11 that God has by no means finished with Israel. He will restore them in the last days. Romans 11:26 states that *"all Israel will be saved..."* He also says that because of Israel's disobedience, we Gentiles have the opportunity to be saved (Ro 11:11*)*. The dynamic is that Israel should become envious of our relationship with God. Paul further declares that this restoration will bring a new wave of blessing to the whole world (v12, 15):

. . . if their transgression means riches for the world...how much greater riches will their fullness bring? (12)

. . . for if their rejection is the reconciliation of the world, what will their acceptance be, but life from the dead? (15)

God also predicted that the Gentiles would have a wonderful and dynamic part in the re-gathering of the Jewish people to their covenanted land (Is 49.22*)*.

In simple terms aliyah means 'to go up' and all pilgrims 'go up' to Jerusalem, which ever direction they come from. Jewish people making aliyah are referred to as 'olim.' How wonderful it is that we should be called to play a significant part in the re-gathering of the people to their covenanted homeland in the last days. Yeshua declares that this restoration is a sign of the nearness of His return (Acts 3:21).

Although there has been an unbroken Jewish presence in the land, the Jewish people began to return in significant numbers in the late 19th century; in part due to persecutions in Tsarist Russia. In 1948 the nation was re-born by the will of God through the office of the United Nations.

An early return following the creation of the state took place in 1949. The Imam of Yemen agreed to let 45,000 of the 46,000 Jews in his country leave by Israeli transport planes.

In 1950 the Iraqi government reversed a ban on Jewish emigration and passed a special bill that allowed Jewish people to leave on condition that they renounced their citizenship. They were also to leave intestate – that is to say, their properties and other financial assets went by default to the state as a condition of exit. Without going into detail, it is worth noting that it caused an internal crisis with the government anxious to get the Jewish people out for anti-Semitic reasons.

In the event, around 121,500 Jewish people returned from Iraq through Operations Ezra and Nehemiah. The Ethiopian Jews began arriving in Israel, as a community, between November 24th 1984 and January 3rd 1985 when a special mobilisation called Operation Moses (in Hebrew, *Meevzah Moshe*) was launched. Some 14,500 Ethiopian Jews, many of whom had succeeded in crossing into Sudan after days of walking from their villages, were flown to Belgium where they were transferred to Israeli planes and taken to Israel. Operation Solomon in 1991 carried a further 11,000-plus from Addis Ababa.

Since the first three Christian-sponsored flights in 1990, Christian agencies have made it possible for around 250,000 Jewish people to return from Russia, Siberia, Ukraine, Georgia, Belarus, Moldova, Armenia, Kazakhstan, Kyrgyzstan, Uzbekistan and Turkmenistan and, more recently, Argentina, Peru, Panama and India. In fulfilment of the Scriptures, these have included the old and young, able-bodied and disabled, the blind and those with child, just as the prophet predicted in Jeremiah 31:8.

Since 1990, over a ten-year period, more than a million Jews have returned to Israel, mostly from the former Soviet Union; more than one third of the total number of immigrants since the foundation of the state in 1948. In the year 1999-2000, immigration rose to a new high with about 73,000 immigrants arriving in the country, of whom 87% were from the fSU. Of this number, around half were brought to Israel through the direct help of Christian-sponsored aliyah.

Israel is the apple of God's eye *(Zechariah 2:8)*, an idiom for the pupil, illustrating the most tender and sensitive part of the Lord's view of things. Thus, the return is both holy and sensitive in His sight. We are privileged to be called to share in this fulfilment of prophecy.

Chapter 2

Christians and the Return: Historical Considerations

During their two thousand years of exile, the Jewish people always held a longing in their hearts for a return to Israel. They said special daily prayers for it and celebrated holidays according to the biblical seasons and calendar. HaTikvah (The Hope), the Israeli national anthem, expresses this historical longing.

The Early Church

The time-frame of the earliest Christian communities following the defeat of the Second Jewish Revolt (132-135) through to the Council of Nicea, called by Constantine in 325 CE, is generally referred to as the Early Church Period.

From the earliest writings of the Church Fathers, there was a marked institutional anti-Semitism: a distinct animosity towards the Jewish people and their place in society. There was also a notable absence of any notion of a future restoration or return of the Jewish people to their land. The vitriolic writings of the leading church fathers led not only to a loathing of the Jewish people in general but also to Jewish believers in Yeshua as Messiah. Jerome, amongst others, despised and dismissed them as being neither 'fish nor fowl'.

Eventually, following the institution of Christianity as the state religion by the Roman Emperor Constantine in 324 CE, relationships deteriorated further, with Jewish people forbidden to settle or remain in the land.

The Mediaeval Church

By the time of the Crusades in the late twelfth century, the Jews were regarded with a developed contempt taught by the church and considered not worthy of life. During the First Crusade in particular, Jewish communities along the Rhine and Danube were destroyed, and once in the Holy Land, the Crusaders massacred Jews without mercy. (see F Wright, *The Cross Became a Sword, The Soldiers of Christ and the First Crusade*)

The Crusades are referred to as the First Holocaust by many Jewish leaders. Meanwhile a hope always burned in the Jewish heart that one day there would be the prophesied return to Zion.

English Protestants

It is during the period of the rise of British Protestants that we first find the notion of return and restoration emerging. The study of the Bible in the original languages, along with the newly-acquired English translations and their availability to ordinary people, led to greater awareness of the Israel of the Old Testament.

Probably one of the first signs appeared in a work of the Cambridge scholar Francis Kett in his 1585 publication, following the literary convention of the day with the wonderfully long-winded title *The Glorious and Beautiful Garland of Man's Glorification Containing the Godly Misterie of Heavenly Jerusalem*. Kett makes a passing comment regarding "the notion of Jewish national return to Palestine" – a notion considered so outrageous and heretical that he was promptly arrested and quickly burned at the stake on January 14, 1589. This for merely entertaining the idea!

Thomas Draxe (d 1618) in 1608 published another book with an even more long-winded title, *The Worldes Resurrection: On the general calling of the Jews, A familiar Commentary upon the eleventh Chapter of Saint Paul to the Romaines, according to the sense of Scripture*. The idea gained momentum and was picked up by Thomas Brightman (1552-1607) and Joseph Mede (1586-1638).

Possibly the most dynamic and influential supporter was the highly respected Sir Henry Finch (1558-1625) who, in 1621, published the still even longer titled *The World's Resurrection or The Calling of the Jewes. A Present to Judah and the Children of Israel that Joined with Him, and to Joseph (that valiant tribe of Ephraim) and all the House of Israel that Joined with Him.*

Finch too was to pay a high price for his endeavour; within a few short weeks he and his publisher were arrested, and he lost his position, reputation, his possessions and his health. King James was offended by Finch's statement that all nations would become subservient to national Israel at the time of her restoration. However, a seed had been sown that continued to hold influence in the centuries to follow.

The Jewish people had been expelled from England in 1290, although there had been several influential, albeit unofficial, Jews in England who were re-admitted on eschatological and financial grounds during the Commonwealth of Oliver Cromwell in 1656.

The 19th century saw a significant rise in support for Jewish people in England by evangelicals such as Lewis Way (1772–1840), a noted barrister and churchman, and founder of CMJ (the Church's Ministry among the Jewish people). Other protagonists included William Wilberforce and, in particular, Lord Shaftesbury who wore a ring on his right hand carrying an inscription that he told colleagues was his daily prayer, *'Oh pray for the peace of Jerusalem.'* Robert Murray McCheyne (1813-1843) was considered a leading authority in his day who, along with Andrew Bonar (1810-1892), Dr Alexander Black and Dr Alexander Keith visited the Holy land in the 1830s. Upon their return, McCheyne published a pamphlet calling the church to recognise the Jewish peoples' biblical right of return to the land.

In the mid-nineteenth century Charles Haddon Spurgeon preached on the return and restoration of the Jewish people (see Appendix 1) while the Wesleys and others wrote hymns on the theme (see Appendix 2).

However, the notion of aliyah as such was in effect an eschatological dimension within their ethos. They believed that the Jewish people would come to faith in Jesus as Messiah through evangelism and, as a result, return to the land of their fathers.

These views, eventually in one stream, led to the Dispensationalism of John Nelson Darby, Cyrus Schofield and his followers, which placed the return and salvation of the Jewish people in a hard-set eschatological framework.

The Niagara Bible Conference in 1878 issued a 14-point proclamation, including the following text:

...that the Lord Jesus will come in person to introduce the millennial age, when Israel shall be restored to their own land, and the earth shall be full of the knowledge of the Lord; and that this personal and premillennial advent is the blessed hope set before us in the Gospel for which we should be constantly looking. (Luke 12:35-40; 17:26-30; 18:8; Acts 15:14-17; 2 Thessalonians 2:3-8; 2 Timothy 3:1-5; Titus 1:11-15)

The USA's founding fathers, the Puritans (literally those who wanted to purify the church), brought with them a burning desire for deeper biblical understanding. Attendant to this was a desire to see the salvation of the Jewish people which in their understanding was inexorably linked with a return to their ancient, covenanted homeland. They gave Hebrew names to their settlements and children. Hebrew was taught at Harvard from 1636 onwards and was at certain times an obligatory course, a policy vigorously promoted by Increase Mather and subsequently President John Adams (1825-1829). The matter was later raised by the so-called father of American Zionism, William Blackstone (1841-1935), who lobbied both Presidents Benjamin Harrison (1889-1893) and latterly Woodrow Wilson (1913-1921) along these lines, encouraging Wilson to support the Balfour Declaration of 1917.

President Harry S. Truman (1945-53) was influenced by his biblical background in deciding to recognise Israel in 1948 in defiance of the State Department's advice, later remarking that it was a Cyrus-like experience.

The effects of the persecution of the Jews under the Romanoffs, the subsequent Russian Revolution and two World Wars not only changed the international map but also the thought and impetus towards their destiny. Much concern got lost in the years of rebuilding following the war. It was not until the 1970s and 80s that we began to see a move away from dispensationalism towards a mass exodus based upon Isaiah 49:22, all of which raised the question of how Christians and Jews viewed each other. The founding of the State of Israel on May 14th 1948 brought tensions into sharp relief both in a positive and a negative manner regarding statehood and its consequences.

The Post War Period

In the UK, CMJ and other Jewish-related missions still worked on what we might term classical evangelisation with no interest in a time of realised aliyah as part of their ethos. The idea of a Christian-assisted aliyah awaited the future as any notion of such an event was temporarily frozen by the Cold War. It also seems, from a careful reading of early biblical Zionist thought, that little attention was ever given to the logistics of how so many people could be transported from a country that was so vast with limited means of transport. Such a scenario would require a huge amount of finance as well as having to navigate adverse weather conditions and mountains of red tape. Neither was there any real discussion of the tensions that would be faced within the land in event of it happening. It may be reasonable to suppose that from the adoption of dispensationalism in the mid-nineteenth century those that held such views were looking for sudden mass conversion followed by an exodus with divine assistance.

The largest part of the world's Jewish population was in the Soviet Union and its satellites, mostly within the Pale of Settlement (see F Wright, *Within the Pale*). Stalin's policy of containment meant that they were pretty much hemmed in wherever they were located. His anti-Semitism verged on paranoia as exemplified by the Doctors' Plot when, in 1952–53, a group of prominent Moscow doctors (predominantly Jews) were accused of conspiring to assassinate Soviet leaders in the Politburo. Initially 37 medical practitioners were arrested but the number soon reached into hundreds with the Soviet media producing a vast amount of anti-Semitic propaganda to back up the spurious claims. **A similar** initiative was undertaken in Poland. The whole matter was abandoned due to lack of evidence within weeks of Stalin's death. Under Nikita Khrushchev there was supposedly a thaw in institutional anti-Semitism. But while mass repressions against Jews decreased, the state closed down the remaining synagogues and introduced further 'religious' restrictions.

The famous Kiev synagogue was turned into a puppet theatre and the press defamed the Jewish religion, Zionism and Israel. There were no Jewish schools or seminaries of any kind in the Soviet Union and none were allowed to be started. In addition, no-one was allowed to be trained to replace the few rabbis that were left. There were no consecrated Jewish cemeteries. The Hebrew language was banned and made a punishable offence if used, in some instances being regarded as seditious. Use of Yiddish was barely tolerated and especially not in public. Any contact with Jews from overseas was harshly dealt with. In the early 1960s a public order campaign known as the 'economic trials' involved a disproportionately high number of Jewish defendants. The nature of the Soviet regime in which state ownership of all capital was a basic ingredient, and every sphere of life had become highly politicised, made economic offences political crimes of the first order. Charges included theft or sabotage of state property, speculation, bribery and other fraudulent practices as well as evasion of work, especially in the Ukraine.

There had been a variety of punishments for economic crimes but in 1961 the death penalty was reinstated for large-scale theft of state property and for the forgery or manufacture of banknotes and securities. Capital punishment was soon applied for dealing extensively in foreign currency, for submitting false economic reports, and for bribe taking. The principal indictments in trials involving Jews were for the 'self-manufacture' of goods, the use of materials stolen or illegally purchased and their sale on the black market, or through state manufacturing offices; also for theft of state property for the purposes of self-manufacture or sale, commerce in gold, precious stones and foreign currency, bribery, and the falsification of documents and reports. Of 84 people sentenced to death for economic crimes in 1962, 54 percent were Jews.

Dark rumours of drunken ribaldry in the synagogues, along with typically crude anti-Semitic stereotypes, were circulated alongside propaganda that the synagogues were sinister places of Zionist intrigues. The term 'Zionism' was in common use and, in reality, stood for world conspiracy, economic conspiracy, treason and American agents. Increasing anti-Semitism and disenfranchisement from many educational and professional areas meant that the Jewish people were largely disadvantaged and impoverished. For instance, their identity papers had 'Jewish' stamped on them, which forbade the issue of certain library books and affected the schools and universities that could be attended, or courses that could be undertaken. In the military, Jewish officers were restricted to lower ranks than others having the same responsibilities. Effectively, over two million Jewish people were deprived of both civil equality and the right to lead a Jewish life.

It is a common error to underestimate what we may term post-Holocaust trauma. Apart from a couple of small essays, there was no major work on the Holocaust until Raul Hillberg's offering in 1964. The rebuilding of Europe, along with the Cold War, were preoccupations in the West where little thought was given to the condition of the Jewish people.

Chapter 3

Christian Awakening

The months between the end of 1963 and early 1964 are a most relevant time-frame with the escalated war in Vietnam, the assassination of John F Kennedy and the subsequent killing of his supposed assassin Lee Harvey Oswald by Jack Ruby two days later. A war between the Greeks and Turks in Cyprus seemed imminent and the PLO became an entity. It was also the year that Christians and, to some extent politicians, became aware of the condition of Soviet Jewry out of which would emerge the beginnings of Christian Sponsored Aliyah (CSA).

The campaign for freedom of emigration from the USSR ('Let My People Go') was started in the very late 1960s, and developed through the 1970s and 80s, by Soviet Jews both within and without the USSR. The first group petitions to be submitted by the *refuseniks* to the Soviet authorities and international organisations were made by Georgian Jews on August 6, 1969, along with those of Moscow, Leningrad and Riga. It is important that, as in the Georgian petition, they were simply seeking permission to return to the home of their fathers; they were not seeking general emigration.

The plight of those in 'the world's largest detainment camp' soon caught the attention of Bible-believing Christians. The slogan 'Let my people go' is an abridged quotation from the Bible. The full sentence reads: "*Let my people go, that they may serve me.*" (Exodus 8:1)

A group that garnered special attention were the so-called *Refuseniks.* These were individuals who studied Torah or were involved in teaching or promoting Jewish culture and the Hebrew language who, upon applying for an exit visa as well as a visa to enter Israel, were refused, usually on grounds of so-called national security. In the West, street demonstrations took place outside Russian embassies and other significant sites. Petitions were raised and fund-raising meetings held. Christian support organisations sprung up such as 'Let My People Go' and 'There is Hope' along with support from Prayer for Israel and the hybrid 'Refusenick'.

The pressure from the West led to a rise in exit visas during the late seventies and early eighties but came to an abrupt about-face with the accession of Yuri Andropov on November 12th 1982. Throughout the Andropov era, short though it was, Soviet Jews suffered in ways unknown for more than a decade. The gates of emigration were slammed shut. From a peak of more than 50,000 in 1979, only 1,300 Jews were allowed to leave the Soviet Union in 1983, and only 88 in the last full month of Andropov's rule. Among the 1,300 allowed out, there were almost no *refuseniks*, no activists, and only a single Hebrew teacher. Andropov's message was clear: the era of emigration was at an end. In his own words, 'the last train had left.'

It was around this time that Steve Lightle's book, *Exodus II*, was published, relating a vision he had received some ten years previously whilst in Braunschweig, Germany, where he was serving with the Full Gospel Business Men's Fellowship International (FGBMFI). The book caused quite a stir and sold a huge amount of copies (for a Christian book). Steve spoke of a forthcoming judgment on the Soviet Union and mass exodus of the Jewish people fleeing by a number of detailed routes. The response to the book was rapid and immense as people started to hold regular prayer meetings while also preparing houses, barns, vehicles and stores of food in readiness for the event. It was interesting that, despite the absence of the routes described, many intercessors had been receiving similar visions from the Lord for a good number of years. As the message spread, there always seemed to be someone who had had the same revelation.

Jay and Meridel Rawling's influential books 'Gates of Brass' and 'Fishers and Hunters' also fuelled Christian interest in the plight of the Soviet Jews and their possible future. An early supporter who put a practical edge upon the matter was Stephen from Edinburgh. Here is Stephen's story:

I first became involved in praying and campaigning for Soviet Jews in the early 1970s. Of course, we weren't really thinking of it then as involvement in aliyah. I heard a woman called Aviva Genden speak at the Edinburgh synagogue pleading on behalf of her husband in Russia. She had been able to make aliyah, but he was held back. At that stage it was almost impossible for the Jewish people to leave Russia. So families were split up. She spoke about her husband and asked people to write to him and to the Soviet government. He was eventually allowed to leave.

I started to pray along with a lady called Elsie Lucas for the release of the Soviet Jews. I was still at school – around 16 or 17. We combined prayer with sending postcards to Prisoners of Zion as they were then called. We collected information from various sources; the Jewish Board of Deputies, Keston College and later the 35s (The Women's Campaign for Soviet Jewry). One of the people I wrote to in these early days was Anatoly Sharansky (now Natan Sharansky) when he was still living in Moscow. I sent my first postcard to the Soviet Union in 1975. We continued with prayer and postcards even though we never had any response. I then travelled to the USSR with my mother in 1985 to visit some of the *Refuseniks*. In total we went four times.

Elsie and I also showed the film 'Prison Land' and formed the Edinburgh Keston College Support Group.

I remember one of the women involved in the 35s saying that "Christians were also being persecuted and no-one seemed to be doing anything for them". We felt that Keston College covered both sides. Later, when the Edinburgh Intercessory Prayer and Action group was formed (also initiated by Elsie Lucas), we followed the same pattern of praying and campaigning for both Jews and Christians.

We hosted meetings and exhibitions, continued sending cards and also supported a programme known as 'Aid to Russian Christians'.

Around this time, I heard Steve Lightle speak in Edinburgh before I read *Exodus II*. It was the first time I had heard anyone put all of this into a prophetic context. I had never seen the things that I was involved with as a kind of prophetic thing, more simply as an opportunity to support Jewish people, especially as I already had an interest in Jewish things as well as an interest in Russia. Steve Lightle and people like him gave me the hope that things would change, and that God would bring the Soviet Jews out. I didn't have a big emotional response, but what he said made good sense and the enormity of it was mind-boggling. When I first heard Lightle, I was getting ready for the trip to Russia with my mother to help and encourage Jewish people. Steve was very encouraging about what we were going to do and prayed for me.

There are some parts of the vision that Steve shared here and elsewhere that have come to pass. Many thousands of Jewish people have left the former Soviet Union, though in reality very few, if any, of the routes have been employed.

On the other hand, a special blessing is that Christians have been involved in aiding aliyah in both financial and practical ways. Given the state of modern Russia, maybe there is still a mass exodus to come and the routes may be employed.

Around this time, I also met Jay and Meridel Rawlings and saw their film (Gates of Brass). The people in the film were excellent speakers, being both measured and thoughtful. The whole idea of 'fishing' was very important as many of the potential olim (emigrants) had been completely cut off from their Jewish heritage and needed a reminder of who they were. It was the first time that many of these Jews had met any Christians who cared about them. Some of the Soviet Jews in the 1970s were both knowledgeable, intelligent and had a sense of purpose which is the reason why many of them were in prison.

Aliyah has now spread far wider than the fSU, which has also affected Israel with Christian-inspired organisations offering a support service to the new olim. It's exciting as isolated Jewish people all over the world are becoming aware of the need to make Aliyah – the Bet Menashe from India, for example. There is a definite ingathering going on from all over the world and it was good to be involved as the Lord began to open the way.

Sister Alice and the Farm

There was a wave of excitement amongst those who supported Israel and the Jewish people following the publication of *Exodus II* and people all over the world began to prepare for the eventuality of Exodus in a number of ways.

Some initiatives were modest, storing dried foods and water tablets, others storing vehicles and various pieces of machinery. Extensions to houses, barn conversions, large tents and field kitchens were also prepared for an anticipated mass exodus from the fSU. Some undertook higher-end cost items such as the purchase and sometimes storage of light aircraft and boats. One brother brought a trailer through Alaska and Canada.

A remarkable early initiative that arose largely outside of direct Western influence emerged in Poland. During the Second World War a young Polish lady who, for personal safety reasons during the Communist period became known as Sister Alice, was increasingly horrified by the treatment being meted out to her Jewish neighbours. She was further alarmed that her fellow citizens seemed determined to hand them over to the Nazi invaders. She had no idea what motivated them – whether greed, fear, hatred or jealousy. Observing the escalating persecution, the horrors of the Warsaw Ghetto and the steady, then increasing, disappearance of those erstwhile Jewish friends, her worries became mixed with shame.

The plight of the Jewish people became a deeply-rooted part of her psyche, forged as it was amidst the horrors of war and the formative sensitivities of youth. When Poland was delivered to the Soviet sphere of influence after the Yalta Conference in 1945, any hope of reparation for the Jewish people disappeared. The thriving Jewish community, which had constituted some thirty percent of the entire population and thus shaped and enriched Poland's cultural life, was virtually extinct. Those who attempted to return were met with anger and brutality and death at the hands of the locals. An example would be the Kielce pogrom on 4th July 1946 when 42 returning Jewish people were massacred by a mob of Polish soldiers, police and civilians in a most grotesque manner.

The young lady in question managed to escape to the West. She found her way to Argentina and subsequently to England where she lived for many years and raised a family. But her burden for the lost Jews of Poland deepened and she wanted to do what she could to care for the survivors. So, following a prolonged season of prayer and fasting, she made her way back to Poland and, aware of the need for secrecy under the ever-present scrutiny of the KGB, adopted the name Sister Alice. At the time of writing the dear lady is over 96 and blind. She reaches out from her apartment in Warsaw to the current team and those who still look to her for wisdom in the current circumstances.

The work began as she gathered a few praying ladies around her. Laying a foundation of intercession, in time they began to clean and tidy long-neglected Jewish graves. Their search for Jewish survivors led them to old people's homes, hospitals and synagogues. Sister Alice and her friends began to serve these elderly, broken children of Abraham, caring for their most basic needs. For years their focus was upon these last remaining Jewish people in Poland.

A new departure occurred as they studied the prophetic scriptures and began to understand that God had significant purposes for these people in the end times. They knew that, though numbers were small in Poland itself, there were millions of Jews in the wider Soviet Union. Their studies led them to sense that persecution and pogroms might once again come to this vast number which could lead to attempts by many to escape and flee the clutches of Communism. Their conclusions were confirmed when Steve Lightle's book came into their possession. Prayer has always been a significant part of Sister Alice's ministry, so once again the little group devoted time to seeking God.

Among other activities, the vision was born for a house of refuge for Jewish families fleeing from the East. The story at this point draws in a young married couple, Gustav and Maria, who feature significantly in the unfolding events. Gustav was a farmer, so the idea was conceived of a farm which might covertly double as such a place of refuge.

It is hard, if not impossible, for anyone who never visited Eastern Europe under Communism to fully appreciate the deprivation and hardship endured by the average citizen. The shops had little or nothing in them, utilities were either broken, rationed or simply not available. The project of finding a suitable property then purchasing it, let alone being able to source building materials, would tax the faith of saints, yet this group believed it was to this they were being called. Around this time in the 1960s, believers from the West began to make exploratory forays into Poland. Under the leading of the Holy Spirit, connections were made, fellowship enjoyed and vision shared.

In the end a suitable small farm with orchards was found east of Warsaw, not far from both the main Warsaw-Moscow highway and the railway from Warsaw to the east. Against all the odds the purchase was made, a working farm established and the countryside scoured for building materials. Quietly, groups of believers made their way to the farm and gave their practical skills to the development. One of many miracles was the discovery of water on a corner of the property, once again in response to prophetic revelation. Following the fall of Communism in the East, believers from the West joined in so that today a large farmhouse stands tucked away in woodland complete with flourishing orchards at the rear of the property capable of housing huge numbers when it might become necessary.

We had the privilege of taking teams to help with the construction of the building in the 1980s, making three visits in one year. The first visit was with a Scottish electrical specialist to design the electrics and arrange for some supplies to be transported in small amounts by visitors from the West. Our major project was putting the roof on. Roy, an American friend and colleague, had experience of this type of roofing and we felt reasonably equipped to undertake the enormous task of putting on the shingles. When we asked where the ladders were, Gustav smiled and pointed to some felled trees and a saw bench next to an extraordinary large pile of shingles, barrels of tar and cases of nails.

We set about making our first ladder with great enthusiasm. The magnificent creation was the full height of three stories to the roof and was of sturdy construction, so sturdy in fact it took four men to lift it and move it to the house.

Whilst the men worked on the roof, Maria and the ladies undertook the task of doing the laundry in cold water and with no detergent! We spent the best part of a month on this mammoth task, enjoying the farm, fellowship, sunny weather and the storks that nested in the trees. That is to say we enjoyed them apart from the clattering noise they made with their beaks at sunrise. We dined on local produce and were thrilled when once a week there was meat on the menu. The evening meal was usually some sort of vegetable stew and occasionally milk soup. As the farm had a good size orchard, apples usually featured in most of the meals. Roy usually asked what the dish was. Maria, with a smile, always gave the same answer: 'Zapiekanka!'

The farm at the time seemed to be a microcosm of the world's heart for the Jewish people and their potential return. There were visitors from Russia, Germany and Israel. The evenings were wonderful times of worship, sharing, planning and scheming for the future aliyah and the subsequent exodus.

In those days building materials were very scarce but somehow Gustav always seemed to be able to resource what was needed at any given time. Poland was a large-scale producer of cement but, as it was one of its few major exports, it was almost impossible to source; needless to say that large amounts were needed. One morning an animated Gustav said the Lord had shown him in a dream where there was an adequate supply of cement available some one hundred kilometers away; no details other than the name of the place. He set off in his truck and arrived back in the evening with a full load!

In a similar manner, vehicle spares were non-existent. About the second week of the trip, a couple arrived from Germany and their VW just about limped into the farmyard. It appeared that a piston ring had broken and there was no local or even nearby agent or supply outlet. To our surprise, the team said not to worry, we can fix it; we have a lathe and can make a new one. The only problem was finding a piece of steel for the manufacture as, along with everything else, there was an acute shortage. Sure enough, three days later a piece of steel was located around 60km away and in no time the part was manufactured and fitted. In a similar way, when our van was broken into in Warsaw, fortunately only one bag with a Bible in it was stolen and the lock was repaired on the street outside a Jewish locksmith's shop using old-fashioned but extremely skilled methods.

For some years, teams from the farm have travelled east to establish networks with pastors and churches, rabbis and synagogues. Many of these have in return visited Poland and learned of the vision for the farm and its availability for the time of need. Following the Chernobyl nuclear disaster of 26th April 1986, Jewish children from the region were invited to the farm for a holiday. Chernobyl is in the Ukraine, but the major fallout was in Belarus in one of the most densely Jewish-populated areas around

Bobruisk. According to official post-Soviet data, about 60% of the fallout was in Belarus. The idea has taken off so that now, all summer long, there are visiting groups of Jewish children having a 'holiday with the Bible' as they are taught their Jewish roots while also enjoying life on a farm. In addition, Bible teachers visit to offer adult teaching.

The full vision for the farm awaits its time, but in the meanwhile the group has grown and multiplied so that now, throughout Poland, there are many similar groups of believers dedicated to prayer, acts of repentance and compassion who keep a watchful eye on both the prophetic scriptures and the unfolding of world events on behalf of the Jewish people.

Chapter 4

Boots on the Ground

The biggest support for the idea of being practically involved in aliyah was amongst the international prayer movement led initially in the main by the late Kjell Sjoberg, leader of World Intercessors, from Sweden. I had the privilege of ministering alongside Kjel on several occasions as well as writing background papers for, and being part of, prayer journeys. A major role was also played by the late Johannes Fascius of the International Fellowship of Intercessors.

The annual International Intercessors prayer meetings in Altenstieg, Germany, became a place of intense prayer and vision for a forthcoming aliyah. These meetings were organised by the late Gustav Scheller who went on to found the Ebenezer Emergency Fund. Steve Lightle, whom Gustav met in 1982, and the late Eliyahu Ben-Haim, who founded Intercessors for Israel, were leading members of this group along with others who undertook prayer journeys into the Soviet Union, particularly to Moscow, to pray *in situ* for the release of the Jewish people and subsequent aliyah. Many others including ourselves undertook prayer journeys to the Soviet Union and its satellites to pray for the release and return of the Jewish people to their God-given homeland.

During 1987 and 1988 we made several trips into Eastern Europe to pray and meet Jewish communities, and spent a lot of time in Poland, Romania, Hungary, Czechoslovakia and particularly East Germany. The latter had one of the hardest line Communist parties and the Stasi (secret police) had cultivated a culture of informants. It is considered that over the years since the construction of the Berlin Wall over 70 percent of the population were informants at one time or other.

Although the intercessors may not have realised it at the time, there was a significant theological shift taking place. The prayers and hopes for aliyah were becoming separated from a dispensationalist eschatological contour that had hung over any potential ideology for aliyah for many years. A mass conversion was not anticipated or expected before the return; the word of the Lord was to be ready and prepare now!

Gustav Scheller, who referred to himself as 'the Swiss Donkey', was one of the first to put arms and legs on the anticipation. As an international businessman he had the skill set required, not to mention the courage to begin to prepare for the practicalities of the event. Gustav's story is well documented in his own book where he writes that in 1991, during a scud missile attack, he got the vision to make these things a reality. In another part of England, the proprietor of a north of England bus company had made similar plans, as had the ICEJ (the International Christian Embassy of Jerusalem).

Mention should also be made at this point of Word of Life ministries then led by Ulf Eckman in Sweden. For some time, they had been preparing a large-scale initiative 'in faith' to take tens of thousands of Bibles and equipment into the Soviet Union when it became possible and embark on a massive church planting programme. The programme was very well thought out as it had provision for a training facility for potential leaders at their Bible School in Uppsala and a potential one in Estonia. In common with all who had lived on the edge of faith, when the dramatic events happened, they were ready and moved immediately.

It is open to debate whether it was fundamental to the initial vision of WOL, but when the Israel contour was included in their mission and concern for the Jewish people was incorporated, the fruit of mission accelerated. Within five years, Ulf Eckman had a clearly defined view of Israel in God's purposes and wrote a book to endorse the work. He shared this at the International Intercessors Conference in Moscow in 1994 that Kjel and I had the honour of being a part.

Early CSA initiatives came from the International Christian Embassy Jerusalem. From their inception in 1980 as a response to the pressure of the Arab oil embargo, the return was part of their thinking. When the thirteen remaining foreign embassies left Jerusalem for Tel Aviv, they remained as an act of solidarity. Howard Flower takes up the story:

On May 28th 1990, in the early hours of the morning, the first ICEJ-sponsored flight of Soviet Jews arrived at Israel's Ben Gurion Airport. As the weary new immigrants descended from the El Al plane to the sound of joyful singing, Christians were waiting, many in tears. Like electricity, the news spread throughout the Israeli media later that day. It was like a prophetic moment in time. The news touched people across the nation and duly spread to Christians worldwide.

The flight was conceived and organised at the International Christian Embassy's National Directors' meeting in Finland earlier that year. Ulla Järvilehto, director of the ICEJ Finnish branch, recounted how it happened: "We had a reps' meeting in Finland, and the Germans had brought along money for Exodus. So we asked Israel's Ambassador to Finland, Asher Naim, about what would be the best way to use it so as to help aliyah. The rest in one sense is history. We would pay for a flight. The Germans agreed; they had money for half a flight, and the Finnish branch paid the other half." This is the story of the very first ICEJ flight named 'Ezekiel'.

By the end of the 1990s, ICEJ had sponsored 54 full airplanes and brought more than 15,000 olim home this way. In the following decade ICEJ would resume the flight programmes by sponsoring both group and individual flights from Finland, Russia, Sweden and France. The Jewish Agency closed their Finland office in 2004 because of budget cuts. The aliyah numbers from the fSU were dropping and much less money was being allocated. Ulla and the Exodus Committee offered to take over full responsibility of aliyah throughout Finland and even pay for the flights, an offer met with many thanks from the Israelis. Now the Finnish route began to operate with charter flights because El Al also stopped direct flights from Helsinki, which made the situation even more complex.

Because so many Finnish people came to visit Israel every year, charter flights were organised. At first, there were empty-leg flights to Israel after the Finns were flown home by the Israeli charter flight so we could buy seats on these empty flights and send the Russian Jews home on them. This worked out well. In the next few years the Finnish airline company tried to minimise the empty legs to economise, so we started putting the Russian Jews on the plane together with the Finnish Christians going to Israel for their pilgrimage and vacation tours. The Christian Zionists were very excited to be bringing Jewish families home to Israel with them. Later, Swedish olim were ready to come on our Finnish flights because of the terrible Muslim anti-Semitism in places like Stockholm and Malmo.

In addition to sponsoring flights, the ICEJ became involved in many other areas of aliyah related work, beginning in 1981 with the Mordecai Outcry, when ICEJ organised demonstrations around the world in support of imprisoned Soviet Jews. When the major wave of aliyah began, ICEJ was involved in helping Russian Jews come to Israel through Finland, sponsoring flights, and supporting buses that brought Jewish people to Warsaw and Budapest. In Budapest the ICEJ Raoul Wallenberg Centre was established as a safe house for Ukrainian Jews on their way to Israel. Later, ICEJ sent a bus from Finland to Uzbekistan to help with the aliyah transportation.

ICEJ began to establish programmes to assist fSU Jews who had emigrated to the USA, Canada and Germany. Canadian branch director Donna Holbrook spearheaded this programme. During an ICEJ meeting in the mountains of Switzerland, Donna related to Howard Flower: "The Lord showed me that Russian Jews will come through Canada on their way to Israel. I spoke with Malcolm Hedding and he confirms this. Where do you think they will come from and how can we help them?" Sometime later and after much prayer I replied to Donna: "They are already in Canada. When a million Russian Jews moved to Israel, another 800,000 moved to the USA, Canada and Germany, just as their forefathers did after the pogroms more than 100 years ago." After the events of September 11th 2001, Russian Jews in the USA and Canada began to move to Israel. Donna organised the programme which is still operating today in the US and Canada.

The first Ebenezer initiative was a Malev flight from Budapest of Russian Jews who had ostensibly been on vacation. The work was a joint enterprise with Keren Heyseod and the newly-formed Operation Exodus. The night before, Gustav Scheller had invited a few people including Gerald Gotzen, Eliyahu Ben-Haim and myself to a meal in a local hotel. After the meal, he shared his vision for a shipping project to bring olim from Odessa in the Ukraine to Haifa in Israel. The announcement was received with great joy by those present and all gave generously to kick-start the programme.

We touched down at Ben Gurion in the early evening, to be greeted by a band along with some government officials. As the aircraft door opened, Steve Lightle erupted onto the stairway, ran down and kissed the ground. The first person off the plane will forever remain in my memory. She was a little old lady aged 83, dressed in a shabby cotton dress, clutching a small red plastic bowl containing all her important things as she emerged into the evening sun. She was presented with a bunch of flowers, a box of chocolates and a copy of the Tanakh. It is unlikely she had ever seen so much chocolate, let alone having a whole box presented to her. She received them with tears in her eyes; she was not alone, there was hardly a dry eye to be seen. This was the first of three flights in early 1991 carrying 720 olim.

From this point there was a surge of energy, particularly in prayer journeying, fundraising, networking, seeking volunteers and preparing training programmes. The proto and early aliyah initiatives were always thoroughly prepared for in prayer before commencement. When I first met Kjel Sjoberg and we became close I used to write background papers for prayer initiatives and support, eventually becoming part of his prayer initiatives. Studying the history and culture of any given location for prayer initiatives is foundational as it is important to clear any spiritual obstacles or history of wickedness, particularly anti-Semitism; unless dealt with, they re-occur. The founder of Chassidic Judaism, Baal Shem Tov, put it this way: 'Remembrance leads to salvation, forgetfulness leads to destruction.'

One of the issues I was concerned about leading up to the first sailings was of the sinking of *MV Struma* some 10 miles off the coast of Istanbul – on the route of the ship. On December 12th 1941 the *Struma* sailed under a Panamanian flag from Constanza in Romania with 769 immigrants who had paid extortionate fees. The vessel, commissioned by the New Zionist Organisation, Beta Israel, and the Irgun, was the last to leave Europe in wartime. Built in Britain in 1867 as a Marquis's luxury steam yacht, it ended up as a Greek diesel ship for carrying livestock along the Danube. Such vessels were known as 'coffin ships' as, due to their age and fragility, they were a tragedy in the making, with stronger ships enlisted for military purposes.

The objective was to anchor in Turkey, and from there to await certificates for entry to Palestine. The *Struma* was mechanically unsound, unsafe, overcrowded and lacked adequate sanitary facilities. The diesel engine was not working adequately so, in the event, a tug towed it out to sea where she drifted overnight. She transmitted distress signals and next day the tug returned, with the crew repairing *Struma*'s engine in exchange for the passengers' wedding rings. The ship got underway again but two days later her engine failed once more and she was towed into Istanbul.

The Turkish authorities prevented the disembarkation of the passengers for fear that the British would not give them certificates and Turkey would be forced to give them refuge. The ship remained in Istanbul for 70 days. The only food and water available for the passengers was provided by the local Jewish community.

Despite appeals from the Bulgarian captain, G T Gorbatenko, that the ship was unable to continue on its way, the Turkish authorities had it towed back into the Black Sea on February 23rd 1942. On the following day a large explosion was heard and the ship went down with a loss of all life except one. Although the cause of the sinking is not definitively known, for a good number of years it was suggested that it was deliberately abandoned near mines. A better assumption is that it was mistakenly torpedoed by a Soviet submarine known to have been in the area at the time. Despite an attempt to locate it in the year 2000, the wreck has yet to be discovered.

The sinking of the *Struma* led to widespread international protest against Britain's policy on immigration into Palestine. The lone survivor, 19-year-old David Stoliar, lived into his 90s after spending many years in Tokyo. In addition, a pregnant woman who had suffered a miscarriage survived by virtue of being allowed to disembark for admission to an Istanbul hospital.

During the first sailings I had the privilege of heading a group of Brits aboard the *Med Sky* in an act of repentance regarding the *Struma*. The captain halted the ship at the spot, accompanied by a blast on the ship's horn to mark the moment. He and his crew graciously attended in full dress uniform and lowered the ship's ensign to half-mast. The Israeli journalists aboard attended, fascinated by this unusual acceptance of responsibility for the tragedy, so much so that one of them led his reportage of the sailing with the story. It was an icy cold wet morning as we gathered at the aft of the vessel to make our act of repentance and hold a two-minute silence. At the end of the two minutes, the ship's horn sounded a long blast, the crew saluted and a large wreath made of flowers attached to pine branches from the Jerusalem forest was dropped over the stern rail. It lay in the water for a few minutes and slowly came apart as all the pieces dispersed. Someone remarked that it was like a symbol of both the memory of guilt and the acceptance of forgiveness that were being exhibited as the components gently drifted apart and moved in every direction.

When we approached the port of Odessa on an icy foggy morning, we could see moving mass in the distance. It was our olim who had been kept outside in sub-zero temperatures. We arrived to a less than warm welcome in more ways than one. Soldiers and Ukrainian officials boarded the ship and immediately restricted the number who could disembark with or without visas.

The port manager was unhelpful and made disparaging comments about rats leaving a sinking ship while the customs officials were deliberately slow and aggressive towards the olim waiting to board. Jewels and precious stones, gold and silver and other valuables were confiscated as they were "not allowed to be exported". Some came on board in tears with minor injuries where such items had been ripped from their bodies. Family photographs were ripped up on the ground of national security, medicines, surgical appliances and wheelchairs were confiscated as they were 'needed in the nation' and even baby formula was taken which caused great distress. Fortunately, we had a medical doctor on board and a good supply of basic medicines and formula.

The port manager suddenly announced that he was not going to allow the ship to refuel or replenish water. He shouted: "If you don't leave, we will tow the ship out into the Black Sea and I hope you all drown!" We called an emergency prayer gathering. A few hours later the late David Forbes of Prophetic Word Ministries along with an American friend and myself stood on the deck to pray and the Lord drew us to Psalm 106. We passed this to Gustav for general prayer and the situation seemed to ease. Within a day or so, the said manager was dismissed on a charge of financial corruption. From this point, progress through customs and documentation speeded up, the ship was refuelled and fresh water, foodstuffs and other essential supplies were brought on board.

On the voyage, the olim were treated to films about the land and talks to prepare them for when they arrived. I enjoyed several hours of sometimes heated debate with the Orthodox Jews who accompanied us and held very aggressive negative views. Their supposed role was to be part of the process and report back to the appropriate bodies. On the outward voyage, their main concern was not to get their own food supplies contaminated by our food supplies, and they insisted that there was no food prepared from proscribed animals and that meat and dairy should not be mixed even for the Gentiles on board. The leader of this group, Chaim, declared at the outset that as far as he was concerned, "This is not Exodus II; this is Holocaust III (the Crusades being Holocaust I). You cannot get away with killing us physically, so are trying to steal Jewish hearts and kill faith and culture." They held a daily 'missionary watch' and tried to persuade secular Israelis, such as journalists and security staff, not to have anything to do with us.

On the way back, a couple of the academics amongst them decided to talk to me and, for three days, we met each evening for around three hours. Their position was (a) Paul was a renegade Jew, a misogynist and anti-Semite; (b) Paul took a Jewish sage and turned him into a Greek god; (c) Paul invented Christianity and set himself up as its leader; (d) The Holocaust was a direct consequence of Christian thought and teaching; (e) Christian evangelism is not about care for the life or soul of Jews but simply a tool for the destruction of the Jewish people whom Christians want to eradicate.

By the end of the three days we were getting on very well at a personal level and there was a glimmer of recognition that we might not be all bad. In a small way it was an encouragement that CSA was a meaningful initiative that would work towards some form of reconciliation between Jew and Gentile despite the blood-soaked history. We parted cordially and I was invited to come and study at their yeshiva!

A small group of us considered that there might be a potential linkage for olim from Romania to travel by train to the Black Sea port of Constanza and either join the ship or employ the route as a separate exercise under Four Corners ministries whom we will meet later. In the event, as the uptake for the second set of sailings was below expectations, it was decided not to proceed as air travel was more viable.

Chapter 5
Ethiopia

The fall of Soviet Communism had a roll-on effect in many parts of the world that were subject to Soviet dominance or influence. For me personally, the most intriguing of these was Ethiopia. Known in the Bible as Cush, the land has one of the longest-standing relationships with ancient Israel. In fact, the Israelite connection may be said to define their history for the most part of their national and spiritual identity. Moses married an Ethiopian wife (Numbers 12:1). An Ethiopian travelled to Jerusalem to worship and was discovered reading the Jewish Scriptures (Acts 8:27).

There are a number of theories as to the origins of the Jewish community, generally referred to as Beta Israel, which means 'House of Israel' in Amharic, a Semitic language that is the most widely spoken in Ethiopia. Non-Jews there refer to them by the contemptuous term 'Falashas' – Amharic for 'landless people' in the sense of vagabonds or strangers.

The theories of their heritage originate in oral history. Oral histories have been proven to have a high level of reliability as they are learned by rote in a similar way to learning times tables at school.

A well-held theory at one time was that the Beta Israel may be the long-lost Israelite tribe of Dan. Further suggestions were that they may be descendants of Ethiopian Christians and pagans who converted to Judaism centuries ago. They may also be descendants of Jews who fled Israel for Egypt after the destruction of the First Temple in 586 BCE (2 Kings 25). They would have fled to Egypt, moving down the Nile River, and eventually settling in the hills of Gondar and Tigray in the northern area of the country.

The most commonly held view by Ethiopian Jews themselves and generally regarded as the founding mythos within the Christian church regards the visit of the Queen of Sheba (Cush) to King Solomon of Israel.

According to the Ethiopian 'Book of the Glory of Kings,' the *Kebra Nagast*, based upon several Torah allusions as well as 1 Kings 10:1-13 and 2 Chronicles 9:1-12, the Queen of Sheba (Ethiopia and Yemen today), during her visit to Solomon, had a physical relationship and, upon return home, gave birth to his son Menelik. As a young man, he became curious about his father and travelled to Israel where he visited Solomon and was appalled by his idolatry. Making a sudden departure, along with a number of faithful Levites, Menelik stole the coveted Ark of the Covenant, bringing it back with him to Sheba's capital of Axum.

From the 7th century BCE up until 330 CE, Judaism was the official state religion of Ethiopia. But then Emperor Ezana converted to Christianity. The Christians subsequently behaved brutally with repressive rule over the Jews until the latter revolted and overthrew their Christian overlords in the 9th century.

When Colonel Mengistu Haile Mariam rose to power in a *coup d'état* in 1974, 2,500 Jews were slaughtered and 7,000 became homeless as a result of his Marxist ideology that encouraged anti-Semitism in its most vulgar form. Many Jews were sentenced to death on so-called conspiracy charges. My contact, a wonderfully wise older man who had served in Haile Selassi's government, had himself been sentenced to death by firing squad but, by miraculous intervention, had lived to tell the story.

In the 1980s, Ethiopia became more Stalinist in its political outlook and forbade the practice of Judaism along with the teaching of Hebrew. Countless Ethiopian Jews were imprisoned on fabricated charges of being Zionist spies, and Ethiopian Jewish rabbis, known as *Kesim*, were constantly harassed by the Ethiopian government.

In a reflection of the Romanoff's policy in Tsarist Russia, the government employed forced military conscription of minors as a form of both passive genocide and ethnic reduction. The initiative took Jewish boys as young as twelve away from their families – size often being the determining factor – to serve in the army. Many desolate parents never heard from their children again. A Messianic believer, now domiciled in Israel, related to me a wonderful story that took place in the year before Operation Solomon. His 13-year-old son was taken in this manner from Gondar in the north, which was the capital before it was transferred to Addis Ababa by Menelek II in 1886. The Lord showed him where his son had been taken, some hundreds of miles away. At this time, internal passports and visas were required for travel in the country. The said documents were extremely difficult to obtain and, without bribery, impossible. But by divine intervention overcoming not only the complicated process and associated red tape, he gained the documents. The Lord directed him to the barracks where his son was held, arriving just as he was about to be taken to a conflict zone. Against all odds and by the Lord's hand and what can only be described as a miracle, he was able to secure his release.

A previous initiative to release Ethiopian Jews was Operation Moses that took place on November 18, 1984 and January 5, 1985 when 8,000 Jews were brought to Israel. In some areas it is falsely considered to have been a knee-jerk response by Israel to a quasi-spontaneous desire for an exodus of persecuted Jewry, encouraged by word of mouth and rumour. The movement came at great human cost. The Ethiopian Jews' only option was to proceed by foot to Sudan by night, whilst hiding during the day from robbers and soldiers. At least 4,000 would perish on their desperate route to make aliyah. Starvation, dehydration, disease and fatigue took their toll, along with the poor sanitary conditions in the refugee camps of Sudan. Many Ethiopian Jewish women were raped, captured and sold into slavery whilst trying to reach their destiny in Israel.

Despite these troubles, a further 1,200 departed in Operation Sheba and 800 more on Operation Joshua that took place in 1985 with the help of George H. W. Bush, then Vice-President of the United States.

In one sense, sadly there was little enthusiasm for the so-called *'falashas'* of Ethiopia amidst the euphoria of the possibilities of a massive aliyah from what was sometimes called the great Jewish prison of the USSR or latterly fSU. It was in some ways due to that great saint, Gerald Gotzen, that I had the opportunity of becoming involved in what, over all these years of working on aliyah, remain among my most treasured memories. Gerald was tragically killed in a road accident in Ethiopia in December 2018.

An invitation led to a visit to Ethiopia in 1990 and again in early 1991, essentially to provide humanitarian aid to the so-called *Falashas*. At the time the land was devastated by famine, disease and civil unrest as the Communist government was struggling to maintain its hold. It was not uncommon to see dead bodies in the street as a result of starvation or leprosy. In the latter case, emaciated bodies with their associated lesions, scarring and subsequent malformations seemed like something from a cheap horror movie.

An American lady, Susan Pollack, who was serving as the resident director for the American Association for Ethiopian Jews, reported in February 1989 that the Jews were in a desperate situation, suffering from polio, tuberculosis, malaria, skin fungi, goitres, skin ulcers and infected wounds. She persuaded the AAEJ to finance the transportation of Ethiopian Jews to Addis Ababa, where they would await documentation, visas and processing for aliyah. It is considered that around 6,000 arrived in Addis under this programme. It was a long and impoverished wait for most of them, and the transition from dirt farming to city life did take its toll in a number of cases. Some of the worse cases involved people living in little more than scraped out holes in the ground with a meagre, often threadbare cover.

At this time, one had to have not only an entry visa for where you were staying, and the choices were minimal, but also get an internal visa(s) if one wanted to travel within the land. Needless to say, these were very hard to obtain but Gerald, through his previous work there, knew the right people and procedure to procure them. Our aim was to visit Gondar, the ancient capital where there was still a significant Jewish presence. The trip by air had its own bizarre dimension. The airport check-in and security were little more than tables where every piece of luggage was checked. The four men in front of me all had a red transistor radio, a bottle of whisky and pistol in their luggage. It was explained to me that these were internal security agents. The pistols had luggage labels attached to them and were hung upon a broomstick handle. After the baggage check, a security interview took place in a rickety, curtained booth where one was repeatedly asked to 'hand over your gun', and it was difficult to convince them you did not have one. Upon being satisfied as to the absence of firearms, the next grilling was about knives or other weapons.

Upon boarding the 'short take-off and landing (STOL)' aircraft, two men entered the cabin with the previously mentioned broomstick handle hung with many more handguns, each with the aforesaid brown luggage labels. To our amusement, they proceeded to hang it on two hooks in front of the two front seats on the right hand of the cabin door which remained open during the flight. One's rapidly receding sense of safety and well-being was not encouraged when the pilot announced we would be flying at only around 600 feet as the entry door would not close properly. The aircraft made a stop at Lake Tana, the headwaters of the crocodile-infested Nile. The flight was full. Nobody disembarked but more people got on and the plane took off with several standing and a few perched on the seat arms. Flying over the world's most crocodile-infested waters in an overloaded plane with the door not properly shut is a great faith booster!

At Gondar we were escorted by police or security everywhere we went. As we proceeded down a road, if it could be called such, we saw a ragged huddle of people at the side of the road in a distressed condition. Upon enquiring who they might be, we were informed indifferently that they were *Falashas*. When further pressed, our informant said they would just stay there until they died because there was no-one to help them and no facilities. Basically; who cared anyway! But we managed to arrange sleeping mats, fruit and water and subsequently transport them in two trucks to Addis Abba to join those waiting to make aliyah.

On returning to the UK, I was greatly moved by the plight of Ethiopia's Jewish people and resolved to help their aliyah in any way possible. They were overwhelmed by poverty, exacerbated by little or no work and no resources. A direct consequence of this is what may be termed the prostitution of desperation. Many girls and women prostituted themselves not because they were immoral, but because it was a choice between that and starvation. There was a reasonable amount of cotton and fabric in Ethiopia, but sewing needles were virtually unobtainable. Along with a contact in our church and particularly my late mother, we set about obtaining as many sewing needles as possible for my next planned trip a couple of months later. PFI were interested in this visit and gave a generous donation in US dollars for the Jewish community in Addis. Due to regulations, all monies had to be declared on entry and departure. But this money and other gifts were carefully sewn into the sleeves of my leather jacket.

At the time, I was principal of a school and tried to fit my next trip around a break. However, when I prayed about it, I felt pressed to go on 20th May. I immediately fought against this date for the assignment as I was far too busy in the time-frame. In the event the only time that could possibly work out was in fact that date. In those days you could only fly to Ethiopia via Moscow, Rome or Frankfurt; the latter being the obvious choice, and the former not being a realistic option as, if there was a delay and you missed the connection, you would have to wait at least two days for another flight. The day arrived and the flight left Heathrow on time, which was important as there were only around 30 minutes to effect the transfer. But the plane landed nearly an hour late and I anticipated that I would have missed the connection by at least 45 minutes, so I was facing a two-day stay-over. However, as we were making the descent, an in-flight announcement asked me to identify myself and approach the front of the aircraft asap. To my surprise, they gave me the first exit from the cabin, and at the foot of the ramp there was a buggy with my baggage that sped me to a waiting aircraft. I was swiftly ushered in and informed that they had upgraded me to business class!

Though I had bought a newspaper at Heathrow, I had not looked at it as I was working on a school matter. As we flew out of Frankfurt, I opened the newspaper to be greeted by a headline that loudly proclaimed the rebels were within six miles of Addis Ababa. It was then that I noticed there were only three of us in business class. I walked to the toilet, which was located on the division between business and the rest of the passengers, to see that on this huge aircraft were only two people in the cabin class!

The flight refuelled in Jeddah, Saudi Arabia, and I assumed that we would be turned back. I reasoned that they were probably obliged to take the flight out, possibly to bring people back from Jeddah. But this was not the case. One man got off there; no-one else got on. We were refuelled and proceeded onward to Addis Ababa.

As we were approaching Addis, we were informed that there was a curfew in place that included a 'lights out' at seven pm. But we were expected to land at 7.30. It was a strange thing to see all the lights of Addis Ababa go out as we approached. Upon landing, we were hurried to awaiting police cars and delivered to our respective hotels. As I began to unpack, I could hear a rumbling noise; as an ex-serviceman I recognised the smell of diesel and cordite – tanks approaching!

I went to reception and was met by a nervous concierge who informed me that there were only three other residents at the Gihon, Addis Ababa's second-best hotel, all of whom had rushed down to see what the noise was. We were greeted by the sound of shelling. The concern was that the rebels would attack the hotel or at least seize it. In the event they passed it by heading towards the Mechanisa which was their main target. Mechanisa is one of the world's largest markets, threaded through with narrow alleys where thousands of people live in cramped, squalid conditions. We watched as the stragglers of the rebel army followed the main contingent, many of them no more than children, several of whom bore severe looking wounds. Many were barefoot and ragged. Throughout the night, the sound of gunshot and the familiar rattles of firing squads and double execution shots haunted the darkness as the smells of war drifted through the night air.

In the midst of all of this, my contact arrived and explained the best way to deal with the situation and how to make contact with home – by hotel telephone in the end. Our focus was to try to reach the Israeli compound and enquire whether we could help move some of the Jewish people living in the city to their comparative safety.

Early next morning, there was a message from the British Embassy asking if shelter was required. I felt disinclined to accept, deciding instead to wait and see. My contact arrived early and we made our way to Mechanisa, although advised by what was left of any security that it was very dangerous as the rebels were making it a centre for their operations.

We were able to help some of the Jewish people in the area to make their way to the so-called 'Israeli Compound' and hopefully some protection. The market area at the best of times was poor and squalid. Now it was even worse with an assortment of dead and sometimes contorted bodies covered in flies and the stench of death. Many old scores had been settled.

Later in the afternoon we were informed that Ethiopian Airways had gathered all their aircraft and fled the country. President Mengistu had also, by pre-arrangement with interested parties, fled to Zimbabwe, taking a vast fortune with him, leaving the country impoverished. We were further informed that all international outbound flights were cancelled as the rebels held the airport. As we stood in a central park, the giant statue of Stalin was being pulled down with joy and celebration amid a party atmosphere. It became apparent that what had been intended to be a few days of compassion ministry was turning into something far more challenging!

The next day began by following the same pattern, when suddenly an excited messenger arrived with news and a request from my contact. His son, who was an air traffic controller named Saloman, was involved in something of great import; and could we go to the Israeli compound as soon as possible. Upon arrival, and also on the way, there was a flurry of activity with young boys rushing around, some barefoot, calling all of the awaiting *falashas* in the area to the compound. Suddenly the sound of aircraft was heard. Groups of people were, for want of a better expression, being 'rounded up' into groups and surrounded by tape to keep them together as they were hurriedly, though in an orderly fashion, being sent to the airport. They were transported in special buses, each with an Israeli soldier of Ethiopian origin on board. The best-kept secret of the time, *Operation Solomon*, had begun.

We worked through the night and the next day, picking up people and taking them to the compound, helping with food and water supplies. We heard some news and rumours, but it was not until the initiative was completed that the enormity and scale of what had happened registered. The top-secret operation saw 34 planes, going on 41 sorties, to bring home to Israel some 14,500 Ethiopian Jews plus five more born in flight.

The background to *Operation Solomon* concerns the deteriorating military situation in March 1991. An 'Envelope Plan' was created by the IDF with the assumption that the Ethiopian government would be willing to co-operate and allow it to proceed. The goal was difficult and complex: bringing 18,000 people to Israel in the shortest time possible. Eventually, by means of a large payment and American influence, the plan got the green light.

In the years following the airlift, aliyah for those remaining was patchy, but the Jewish Agency and others gathered them to a compound in Gondar where they introduced a feeding programme for over 2,000 people along with some training initiatives. As usual, one of the bigger problems concerned documentation. People went off the radar very quickly and it was not uncommon for a man to have been married (or not) and have children with three or four different Jewish or non-Jewish women. This raised a multitude of questions about who could, and could not, make aliyah due to the question of who was rabbinically Jewish – an issue that became increasingly vexatious. A man's claim to aliyah could be based upon being married to a Jewish wife, previous to the current situation, or he was Jewish and the wife or wives were not, which obviously had a knock-on effect on the status of children involved along with legal guardianship, if any.

To all intents and purposes, the Ethiopian aliyah has officially ended with the return of just over 100,000 members of Beta Israel domiciled in the land, aided mostly by CSA and in particular ICEJ.

On subsequent trips to Ethiopia following *Solomon* I was touched by the arrival of the olim at the airport. The flights were generally in the evening when it was dark. The olim arrived dressed in white clothes that are considered suitable for a wedding. From a distance and, as they approached, they appeared as a flock of white doves descending, singing joyful songs as they arrived.

The North American Conference on Ethiopian Jewry were very concerned about a group generally referred to as *Falash Mura*. They were descendants of Beta Israel who were forcibly converted to Christianity in the late 19th century but virtually unknown until *Operation Solomon*, when a number attempted to join the departees and were turned away. The estimated 20,000-26,000 *Falash Mura* said they were entitled to immigrate because they were Jews by ancestry. The Israelis at the time saw them as non-Jews, since most had never practiced Judaism and were not considered by the Beta Israel as part of the ongoing situation. However, they began to provide humanitarian aid to the group in Addis who had been declined and were unable or unwilling to return to their homes. Once it became known that food and medical care had become available, more *Falash Mura* left their impoverished lives in the villages and headed for Addis which immediately put enormous stress on the limited resources of the organisation.

The Joint Distribution Committee, on becoming aware of the situation, provided additional assistance but with the understanding that their action was on a humanitarian basis only. It was made clear that whilst accepting the NACOEJ contention that they were Jews and thus had a right to make Aliyah, there was no ongoing commitment. As the number of *Falash Mura* in Addis grew, the Israeli position hardened. The official view was that these people were not Jews and, if they had ever been Jews, it was in the distant past, and that most were now practicing Christians. They simply wanted to get out of Ethiopia by any means possible and saw an opportunity to escape by claiming to be Jewish and thereby earning the right to immigrate to Israel. The Israelis were convinced this motivation would encourage tens of thousands – perhaps most of the Ethiopian population – to claim Jewish heritage. The situation was not helped by the fact that many, especially women, had crosses tattooed on their foreheads! Israel eventually granted entry to those who were Jews through matrilineal descent and could meet the criteria of the Law of Entry in 2003 which requires them to undergo conversion upon arrival in Israel. So in April 2016, the Israeli government approved a plan to bring 9,000 *Falash Muras* to Israel over the course of five years.

There have been further ICEJ-sponsored flights, with 80 Ethiopians brought home in the first weeks of 2019.

Chapter 6

Siberia – Four Corners

Following the Russian Revolution of 1917, the Jewish people posed a dilemma to the new regime as, theoretically, nationalism or national identity outside of the one-state idea was considered to have come to an abrupt end and belonged to a past phase of history. In a similar vein, religion had also reached an end.

However, Lenin and some of the other early Bolsheviks reluctantly came to the realisation that, in general, people remained attached to their national and ethnic identities and these tensions could not simply be abolished by decree. Lenin and his colleagues decided to give a measure of acknowledgment to the tension in a minor way, assuming that the entire national-ethnic contour would eventually diminish into obscurity under the emerging pan-Soviet ideology.

The notion at least to give some minor nod of the head to ethnonationalist, or maybe more properly, sub-nationalist, aspirations was at first considered to be fairly straightforward as most nationalities or ethnic groups were distributed in a relatively compact fashion. Inevitably, however, as history had borne out, there was one group whose mere existence caused the whole process to come into question – the Jews.

Prior to the revolution, most Jewish people were largely limited to towns and villages within the Pale of Settlement (the Baltics, Poland, Moldova, Ukraine and associated territories). The more successful amongst them, despite huge disincentives, penalties and pogroms, had managed to settle and thrive in the major cities of Kiev, Nikolayev and Sevastopol, a minority becoming very successful in trade.

The leadership came up with a strategy that would, when implemented, have severe consequences in the succession period, and immediately following the post-war era. The notion was to resettle all Jews in a defined geographical identity where they would be able to enjoy a lifestyle that would be socialist in content and national in form.

In a revoltingly similar way to Hitler's later supposed search for a final destination for the Jewish people to relocate and pursue a national identity (Madagascar for instance), a location was sought. The first area considered for resettlement was in the Crimean Peninsula, which already had a sizeable Jewish population. However, fearing that this would ultimately lead to the rise of a potential Jewish powerbase, the idea was put aside. Instead, a cynical plan was drawn up and implemented to relocate the Jewish people into a remote part of the Russian Far East, bordering China's Heilongjiang province, around the city of Birobidzhan, Siberia. The area has a monsoonal climate with warm, humid summers and a high density of mosquitoes, along with extremely cold, dry and windy winters. It was a most inhospitable place to settle that would inevitably increase mortality rates and provide a hard standard of living.

To encourage Jewish migration, a massive propaganda campaign was introduced, including posters and novels describing a socialist utopia. Leaflets were dropped from aircraft over Jewish areas and a government-produced film called *Seekers of Happiness* told the spurious story of a Jewish family fleeing the Great Depression in the United States to make a new life for themselves in Birobidzhan. The film had a degree of success with some 1,400 immigrants from the United States, South America, Europe and British-mandated Palestine making their way to Birobidzhan to partake in a forlorn hope.

So there was clearly a need to visit Siberia and the Birobidzhan area to meet community leaders and make arrangements wherever possible to facilitate aliyah. Following the first sailings, at a conference in Jerusalem in 1992 where I was drafted in to take a couple of sessions, I re-encountered an American businessman who prefers to remain anonymous. He had been a major sponsor of the ships and I had shared a cabin with him. He had also been a close associate of Steve Lightle. Following the sailings, Steve took some time out of ministry and asked us if we could use a small depository of funding for an aliyah project. The businessman had access to around $40,000 left in Steve's ministry and it was suggested that we took up the said residue as Four Corners Ministry for an Aliyah-related initiative. My friend, who lived in Alaska, asked me to consider working with him, and he would also finance an aliyah project in Siberia and particularly Birobhidzan. It was envisaged that the plan would be two-fold; firstly, an airlift followed by a land route over the Illushin Islands in winter and down through Alaska and Canada when aliyah turned to exodus.

The team expanded to four when joined by two professional country singers from Texas. Joy and Stella had heard the call of the Lord during the Lebanon conflict and went to Israel to join a support unit for the IDF. On the back of this, they had been allowed to stay in Israel and work on various relief projects. So we would do the work in Siberia and they would do the work in Israel to facilitate the arrival of the olim.

In Siberia, we were delighted by the response from the local churches which, at the time, were in the main only two or three years old. One of the leaders, Alex, had set up a security company and was prepared to help where needed including organising the collection and transportation of the olim. It didn't take long to find potential olim – from Birobidzhan, Magadan and the Khabarovsk regions – and the JA authorities quickly provided the paperwork. In terms of documentation, it may have been one of the most straightforward as everyone's papers were to hand locally. In Moscow we had the usual drawn-out procedures for such an initiative, but they also proved to be reasonably drama-free.

The first problem we encountered was the usual one in that there were no scheduled international flights to Israel from either Magadan or Khabarovsk. Happily, Aeroflot said they would be prepared to hire us an aircraft and provide a flight for the purpose. Initially, we would have preferred to use Alaskan Airlines or an American airline and were not keen to use Aeroflot as we had gained permission for other airlines to use Khabarovsk for a flight. Because of the vast distance, the initial idea was to fly via the USA for re-fueling, but access to US air space and landing for refueling were denied on the grounds that the passengers in question may refuse to leave the USA by claiming asylum. So we were left with the single option of flying Aeroflot – via Samara in Russia for refueling.

The day came and we prepared to leave Anchorage (in Alaska) later that evening on a transport plane to Khabarovsk that had a few passenger seats. Around eleven in the morning, while it was still dark, we got a phone call from Khabarovsk saying that the previously arranged cash payment of over $200,000 would not be allowed and they wanted it paid in American Express Travelers Cheques. We phoned the bank who at first thought we were joking! But as my friend was a well-known businessman in the small community, they said they would do what they could to help. Alaska, then as now to a degree, is a massive land mass with a very small population. Due to banking hours and distances, the bank said they would try to get all the travellers' cheques they could acquire before they closed. The hours and minutes slowly ticked by and just before the closing, they informed us that they had managed to get the full amount. We rejoiced greatly. There might, however, be a small problem, they informed us, as apart from just a few at one thousand dollars, the rest of the cheques were in hundreds, fifties and twenties but mostly tens and fives. So we sat down for a mammoth signing. A couple of hours later we were surrounded by a huge pile of cheques spilling onto the floor. The bank had no container for them, so we left carrying them in a shawl donated by one of the tellers!

The flight was uneventful and on arrival, as there were no hotels, we stayed in the pilots' accommodation where we met our pilot for the following day. Pavel was the chief pilot of Aeroflot's Far Eastern division. The next morning, following a breakfast of four fried eggs swimming in grease and red caviar, we met Alex and his crew who escorted the hired buses and around 300 olim to the airport where they began to make their way through customs. We had put some money up for extra customs and admin staff and, to our surprise and blessing, the process took a reasonable amount of time without any issues arising. The only problem was that there were seven more passengers than seats. We also had what, from the earliest days of aliyah, were the usual accompaniments of dogs, cats and other pets including a parrot, along with a huge amount of musical instruments. At least we did not have horses and pianos on this occasion! The authorities were not bothered about the surplus passengers who arranged themselves with small children on their laps so everyone had a seat and we took off for Eretz Israel. The flight remains the only one I have been on where they actually cooked the food by bottled gas, on board, in a galley in the middle of the aircraft in large stewpots.

After an uneventful flight, we landed in Samara for refueling, cleaning and restocking water, food and so on. Within minutes we received a demand for $20,000 for the service. When it was pointed out that this had been paid for and the documents shown, the airport manager insisted this was nothing to do with the regular payments; this was a service charge. We prayed about this and made the decision that we would not succumb to the demand, as a result of which we received a number of threats. The pilot was furious and demanded a meeting. So we disembarked via rope ladders for a conference on the tarmac, whereupon the pilot told us to get back on the plane and got into a vehicle and vanished into the night.

The minutes turned to hours and the aircraft had neither heating nor water – not even to flush the toilets. By some miracle all the children slept through this and even the parrot remained quiet. Six hours later the pilot returned to say, "We may have enough fuel to fly to Moscow. If we fly low, slow and pick up the main roads in case we have to make an emergency landing we should be able to do it." As we approached Moscow it was obvious that we were in a bad way, but the pilot got it onto the tarmac where fire appliances and ambulances were waiting in case of a 'fuel out'.

A representative of Aeroflot immediately boarded the plane followed by a cleaning crew and baskets of bread, fruit and water. Within an hour, the plane was refueled and re-watered and we took off on our diverted route to Israel. As the lights of Moscow turned to dots, the Chazan of Birobhidzan and the community leader walked the length of the plane with a Channukaot (nine-branched menorah) that was nothing more than a folded piece of steel with nine points to hold birthday-type candles and sang the Channukha liturgy; it was the last day of the festival.

As we approached Tel Aviv, a great problem arose that we had not considered. As we had missed our landing window by some seven hours and it was now two o'clock in the morning, the airport was closed! Various ideas were posited, such as diverting to Cyprus or considering if a further four hours circling may be an option, but air traffic basically said that these were not options. Panic. But then, suddenly, we received a message that Ben Gurion would open to receive the flight after all.

We duly landed and our precious cargo alighted some twenty-four hours after we had taken off. The aircraft was greeted by a small party of officials who whisked them off to an absorption centre to be processed as the airport was still officially closed. My colleague and I stood on the tarmac not quite sure what to do as all the doors into the terminal were locked. A security officer approached and informed us we were not allowed to be in the airport, and especially not on the airfield, as in those days there was quite a large military presence. On being asked what we should do, he shrugged his shoulders and gestured for us to follow him. We approached a small side gate which he unlocked and left us standing outside without a passport stamp and no means of getting anywhere. We walked round to the front of the terminal and towards the car park hoping there may still be a taxi, or that we may be able to call one. To our immense relief, Joy and Stella were waiting there – as they had been doing for around nine hours!

Two days lays later I set off for the journey home with some trepidation; to be in Israel without an entry stamp on your passport was not a good idea, especially at that time. When I met the security interviewer, there was an immediate call for a senior officer and I was escorted to the special interview room. I explained what had happened and was informed that it was impossible. So I showed them the flight manifest, only to be informed that this particular flight did not arrive. I insisted that it had and he went off to check. Around ten minutes later I was greeted with profuse thanks, passport stamped and escorted to the VIP area for coffee and a pleasant, if somewhat bemused, conversation about CSA, and then an hour or so later when the flight was called, I was driven over the tarmac to the aircraft where I was upgraded. It was Christmas Eve.

Tragically, Joy and Stella were both killed in a motor traffic accident in the USA some months later while on a singing tour to raise funds for aliyah.

Chapter 7
Belarus

Two other early initiatives of Four Corners were to have unexpected results. While organising the Siberia assignment, we also had a request to visit Belarus to see if we could encourage and facilitate aliyah. Before World War II, the population of cities such as Minsk, Pinsk, Mahiliou, Babrujsk, Viciebsk and Homiel was more than 50% Jewish. In 1939 there were 375,000 Jews in Belarus, or 13.6% of the total population. But some 246,000 of those (i.e. 66%) were killed during the Holocaust. Anti-Semitic attacks on the remaining Jewish communities had increased since independence. In Minsk in particular, Jewish people had been attacked in their own homes. Some had been forcibly ejected from their apartments with locals moving in. An elderly man was thrown over the balcony to his death from several floors up. In Babrujsk, there were severe problems of poverty and supply, in the main due to fall-out from Chernobyl landing in the area. In Viciebsk, home of the famous artist Marc Chagall, the Nazis and their collaborators had set up five death camps, killing one in three of the population, and the city remained a hotbed of anti-Semitism.

Faced with this challenge, I set out by train from Odessa where I was working at the time, accompanied by my translator, a Russian Gypsy and assistant professor of literature named Voldymyr who was working on a tri-lingual version of the New Testament into Russian, Romany and Polish. The trains were not the most hygienic as well as being very slow, taking around 22 hours. We visited Viciebsk and, through local believers and the Jewish Agency, made some contacts who were keen to make aliyah. But there was no easy route out, in addition to which some locals had got wind of what was happening and were very resentful that Jewish people could leave and they could not. The plus was that they had the documents needed and exit and entry visas. At first sight it looked like being quite straightforward, at least in these matters. Babrujsk was a different story, however, with questions regarding health issues and transportation to an exit point. In the meantime, we were able to provide short-term help with food and other needs.

Our last meetings were in Minsk where we stayed with a professor of literature and his wife, a professor of zoology. At five-thirty in the morning the prof said he wanted to talk to us, and would we join him for breakfast – a remarkable feast of blinis, caviar (red), smoked fish, sour cream, vodka and brandy! He was very interested in what we were doing and, although neither Jewish nor Christian, said he would try to help in terms of contacts for anything we needed. In those days a church would normally have been planted by a group called New Life whose churches usually met in apartments as there were no real facilities. It used to amuse us that when one of these churches was set up, they were supplied with a fax machine and other electronic devices that could not be used as well as a keyboard for worship.

Minsk, however, being the capital with a decent-sized congregation of about 120, had their meeting in a social club. I spoke and explained about the call of the Gentiles and aliyah. The meeting went well, but it was clear that some were uneasy at the thought of being personally involved. The pastor was warm and said he would try and organise transport to help with their departure. He introduced us to a lady (the one who had invited us and was among the leaders) and she asked us to come back to her apartment to meet a group who had been praying for aliyah and for Israel in general. We got to the apartment and had a wonderful time of sharing and prayer. She said that her husband would be home soon and would be really pleased to meet us. However, could we please excuse him as he was not yet a believer and would probably have had a lot to drink. The door opened and an imposing man in evening dress entered smoking a large cigar. He welcomed us and explained he had just finished a recital and that he was a principal at the conservatoire. After we had talked for an hour or so, he asked if we would like to hear him play the piano. There was no piano in sight. But he walked over to a set of ceiling-to-wall curtains and pulled them back to reveal a Steinway grand piano replete with candlesticks, with candles that he lit. He turned off the lights and proceeded to play the Moonlight Sonata and a couple of other pieces. It was an experience I will never forget. When he finished, by which time it was around two in the morning, he questioned us intently about what we were doing and said he had never given religion much thought – until now. The group gathered in the apartment pledged to give as much help and resource as they could. So far so good. We had the people; we had the facilities for documents – now how could we get them to Israel?

This was still of course the very early days of CSA and transportation from the fSU to Israel was in its infancy. My American businessman friend had contacts with Air New Zealand. LOT, the Polish airline, were rapidly expanding and had ordered some Jumbo Jets, and Air New Zealand had sent at least one along with instructors. He had discovered they had some down-time and would have been prepared to have a charter from Minsk to Tel Aviv. However, there were two problems, as we were to find out. Firstly, Minsk was not an international airport, and secondly, a contract had been signed that restricted the carrying of olim to specific third parties! In the event, those we gathered from this initiative were transported from Warsaw. An aside to this story is that Minsk was raised to international status very soon afterwards – and one of the first flights was to Tel Aviv.

In the same time-frame, I was invited by an American pastor to accompany him to Kobryn, near Brest, Belarus, where several new churches that had been founded by an American evangelist wanted Bible teachers to visit. I accepted the invitation on condition I could speak on Israel and the Gentiles' responsibility to aliyah. It seemed opportune as I had recently returned from there and it looked like a good exit point for aliyah by train to Warsaw. The plan was agreed but to my surprise they wanted me there within the next couple of days. I pointed out that it would take a few days at best to get a visa. They told me that I could get one on the border. I admit to having doubts.

We met up at Warsaw and duly took the train to Brest. When we arrived at the border, all the Poles were told to get off the train. The guard came into the compartment and asked for passports. Of course, I did not have a visa. Without moving the obligatory cigarette from his mouth, he said 'valuta' – basically saying 'pay for visa'. I answered in the affirmative and he took my passport, gestured to me to stay where I was and disappeared.

I knew that we would be at the crossing point for some time as they have to change the wheels on the train because, in Belarus, the gauge is different to that in Poland. To my surprise, however, the train pulled away and my passport had not been returned. Being in any fSU country in the very early days without a passport was a recipe for disaster. The Lord, however, knows all things and does all things well. There was something for which we had been ill-prepared that was to make a great difference to what might have been.

We duly reached our destination and, with some trepidation, I opened the train door to find the same guard standing there holding my passport. He signaled us to follow him and we reached the station hall to find it crammed with hundreds of people and piles of baggage. The guard indicated we should wait. We found a payphone and rang our contact who said it would probably take about three days to get through immigration and customs! "We had expected that you would have got here a few days earlier to allow for this," he added.

Shortly afterwards the guard escorted us to the visa checkpoint, asked for two dollars and, a few moments later, returned, accompanied by another guard wearing something akin to an ice-cream sales harness, except with stamps and an ink pad. He asked for the fee and stamped the passport. The guard asked for another two dollars and escorted us to the front of the queue for visas, stayed with us and then escorted us through customs without any checks. He then spoke to us for the first time in good English and said if wanted the same service on the way out he would give us a number to call at the station. One dollar for the number and five dollars for the person who would take us through, to be paid to said person at the time.

We held a number of meetings sharing about Israel in God's plan and the return of the Jewish people. These meetings were hard-going as a lot of them did not have full Bibles – only New Testaments. However, we were able to introduce the groups to others in Poland and encourage them to start reaching out to the Jewish people and bring reconciliation and help with aliyah.

On the way back, we duly phoned the number flagged up and, for $5, were escorted straight through to departures. The churches there subsequently grew, and an appreciation of the role of Israel and aliyah in God's economy became foundational in many.

Chapter 8

The Work Begins in the fSU

Along with Michael Utterback and myself, Pat is the longest serving worker in CSA. From her earliest involvement, she has worked as Field Director for Ezra International, in addition to pioneering new areas. Here is Pat's story:
I first became aware of aliyah somewhere in the mid-1980s, first of all through reading Steve Lightle's Exodus II. When I read the book, I wasn't sure about it, but it affected me very much and, when I finished reading, I got down on my knees and prayed, asking the Lord that if this was true, would He show me from His word; and if it was true, would He show me what He wanted me to do. I began to see all these Scripture verses about the 'land of the north' which I'd really not noticed before! Not long after I read the book, Steve Lightle came to Edinburgh and I went along to that meeting with a friend. To be honest, I couldn't take him too seriously as he reminded us both a bit too much of comedian Ronnie Barker! But I remember one of the young men praying concerning the Aliyah and it was very powerful, and I know that God touched my heart.

After Steve's visit to Edinburgh one lady, Elsie Lucas, established a prayer group to pray specifically for the return of the Soviet Jews. She had already been praying for this for some years. When I arrived at the first meeting, I felt as though I had landed somewhere in outer space – I really didn't understand what people were talking about and it all seemed pretty strange, but I kept being drawn back. Through these meetings I began to learn much more about the situation for the Soviet Jews ('Refuseniks'). Two of the group travelled into Russia several times to meet with the Refuseniks and I also learned a lot from them. The group (EIPAG – Edinburgh Intercessory Prayer and Action Group) met officially only about once every quarter, but it gradually took up more and more of my time in various ways. We not only prayed, but also campaigned for the Soviet Jews. We did postcard campaigns – highlighting the story of one individual or family at a time, sending them to the Soviet Ambassador in the UK requesting exit visas for them, and of course, we prayed. I don't remember now how many we campaigned for, but I do remember we had 100% success rate. We even used to hold annual open-air meetings in the centre of Edinburgh where we read out the names of Christians in prison for their faith in the Soviet Union and of Jews who were refused exit visas.

Some of the group were more inclined to prepare for Soviet Jews coming to Scotland and were collecting supplies (but not in a huge way). I felt then, as now, that it was important to find out their current situation and do what we could to help. I felt that, with this attitude, if and when they did arrive here, we too would be prepared. A few of the group started to learn some basic Russian words.

A couple of years later I saw an advert in the Scotsman newspaper, which I very rarely bought, for a post-graduate course in the Russian language. I was very drawn to this. That same evening a friend phoned me saying she'd seen an advert I might be interested in! So I applied, didn't tell anyone, and within three weeks received a conditional offer (I only had to prove my qualifications). I left my lecturing post and undertook the nine-month intensive course in Russian; the hardest thing I've ever done!

I determined early on that, having worked so hard to get this qualification, I needed to use it in the future. By God's amazing grace I ended up working in Holland for three years with a Christian organisation working to help persecuted believers in many countries. My area of responsibility was the former Soviet Union. It was a tremendous privilege to serve these brothers and sisters and to meet so many of them. In those days I could only travel once or twice a year to avoid arousing suspicion. Amazingly, many of the main contacts also happened to be Jewish, ranging from Pentecostal to Russian Orthodox! That led to many interesting conversations and insights. Part of my job was to send in other 'travellers' to collect up-to-date information and debrief them upon their return. One of those 'travellers' was James from the UK who once asked me, 'Pat, if you ever hear of someone working with the Soviet Jews would you let me know?'. I agreed, on the basis that he would do the same. Within the year he had heard, through someone else, of Phil Hunter and Exobus. Through that connection, four Russian speakers joined the team in Hull; James and his girlfriend (now wife) Ruth, me and a guy from Holland, Sib.

I think God used Exodus II to stir up an awareness of aliyah and kick-start a real move to help, particularly the Soviet Jews at that time. I had some concern even back in the 80s that people were 'waiting' for an event (the expulsion of the Jewish people) rather than doing what could be done for them at that point in time. This is still my feeling. I believe that if we help now in whatever way we can, we will be in a better position to help as things change in the future. Right now the Jews of the fSU (and those in other nations) have a freedom to leave without being forced. We have an open door to help them and I believe we should use this opportunity to the maximum. God also used this book to raise up prayer for those areas, which broke up the ground when the various aliyah ministries started to work. There is not that same foundation of prayer for the other nations, but God promised he would bring them from the land of the north and the other nations. I think that sometimes people have looked at the vision more than at what the Scriptures say and there's always a danger in that. I remember many years ago one woman almost heckling at a meeting, saying we needed to get back to the original vision, advocating that people should walk from the Soviet Union to Israel as that would be fairer! I really don't know how she worked that out but anyway my response was to say, yes, we needed to go back to the original vision and look more closely at what the Scriptures have to say on the issue!

An interesting dimension of the early days was that it was a new initiative and, with the exception of the first Exodus, had no real precedents and certainly nothing remotely similar from which to draw. So Pat was absolutely correct in saying the Scriptures were the operations manual, and prayer was communication with the Lord as CEO, so to speak, in this situation. The former Soviet Union and satellites were in chaos and a state of virtual anarchy, not to mention financial instability; many people, in particular those who worked directly for the government in education, medicine and administration, had not been paid for months in some areas, and especially in smaller towns where bartering ran as a secondary form of trade. Then, as now, documentation provided major tensions – not just passports, but exit and entry visas, proof of identity, permissions from third parties whether government or family related, along with the mass of paperwork for vehicles, internal travel and other things that seemed to be made up by petty officials as they went along.

Two unexpected issues arose that would cause us to smile later but were immensely challenging at the time. One day, the Exobus office in Kiev received a most unusual request. It started off as an ostensibly routine matter with a lady asking for transport from a city in the east of Ukraine to the airport in Kiev. Then she said, 'There's just one problem; I want to bring my husband with me.' On the face of it that didn't seem to be an issue, but she went on to explain that he had been dead for just over ten years! Fair play to her; this lady had taken a great amount of initiative. In the early post-Communist period when people were so used to having all areas of their life governed and controlled, she had sought and received permission to exhume her husband and take his remains with her to Israel. On her departure day she travelled with other olim in one of the buses, but a driver and van were sent to pick up her husband who was travelling in a large metal box. Our driver was a Danish man, Erik, who spoke poor English and no Russian.

As often happened, the van was stopped by the police on its journey to the airport. They wanted to know what was in the back of it. Erik didn't have the words to answer them, so he mimed slitting his throat and then crossed himself. Fortunately, the police got the message and quickly waved him on. Once at the airport he was able to drive right onto the runway and up to the plane itself where his cargo was loaded directly onto the aircraft. This story became known as 'Jacob's Bones' and was just one of the issues that had to be dealt with concerning the deceased.

I well remember sitting round the table in 'Beit Jim' (the flat where most of our drivers lived and where the team ate communal meals together) discussing and writing the policy of what to do if someone died on the coach. The subject was becoming a pressing issue following three deaths within a few weeks of each other – all elderly people in poor health.

The first time this happened, the drivers and courier weren't sure what to do and drove on to the airport with the body on the back seat. But they soon discovered that this was not the best course of action! It caused a huge amount of red tape that had to be sorted out. The families in all three cases had to make the distressing and more or less instant decision on whether or not to continue their journey or stay on to bury their loved ones. Within a few weeks we had two further deaths on separate journeys and the right procedures were decided upon and followed!

Volunteers, particularly on the bussing project, tended to be younger people. They were dedicated, brave and came from a variety of countries and backgrounds including the UK, Germany, Holland, USA, Bulgaria, Slovakia, Ukraine, Belarus and Russia. Here are some of their stories. One of very first volunteers was James from the UK:

I first become aware of the aliyah movement during my childhood in the mid-1970s. As a family, we prayed both for persecuted Christians in the Soviet Union and the plight of the Jewish people who desired to leave and were trapped. I became increasingly aware of Jewish people and their desire to return to their ancient homeland. I first became involved in aliyah following a meeting with Steve Panchaud, and subsequently joined Exobus, also known as Good News Travels, in 1991.

When the day arrived and we found ourselves on the field, we were immediately faced with some big practical challenges such as getting fuel for the coaches. In those days, garages as we understand them hardly existed; fuel was often sold from containers on the side of the road and, assuming you found a supply, it could often take hours or even days queuing before getting it. We would spend days searching for it. At one time we were short of fuel and didn't have enough to get to Warsaw. [At that point we were taking olim from Ukraine to Warsaw as there were no direct flights to Israel from Ukraine.] A little Zhiguli car pulled up and we asked the driver if he knew where to get 300 litres of diesel. It just so happened that this guy's little car was literally full of 20 litre cans! I saw it as God's provision and we were able to make the purchase we needed.

Along with keeping the vehicles fuelled and in good repair, another major tension was keeping to time schedules as the condition of the roads was very poor; on some stretches the surfaces had worn away completely and were full of holes, some of them quite deep. However, a major hindrance was that the police, and particularly the GAI (traffic police), loved to stop us for any reason – whether on account of the officialdom that dominated everything or for on-the-spot fines which could usually be negotiated as they were seen as perks that went into their own pockets. There was a challenge to everything you did. The Soviet Union had been very structured and worked on what we might call a downward spiral of domination, control and abuse. One of the reasons I felt my time there was over was when I realised that I was beginning to think like the Soviets; your sense of what was right and wrong gets very warped.

The first trip out to Warsaw carrying olim took place on the 23rd June 1991. We had to use Warsaw for air transportation as there were no flights or possibility of flights from Russia or the Ukraine. The initial plans were to drive to Budapest or Vienna; GNT (Good News Travels) was under contract at the time with the Jewish Agency and they requested that Warsaw be the exit point. I was the courier on this occasion.

We had 18 olim on board. We set off on that trip, having been told by Phil Hunter, founder and director of the ministry, that everything was arranged at the border. Of course, it wasn't really. There was one official, Nikolai, who travelled with us and he did sort things out somehow. On that bus there was a blind man, a man with one leg, a pregnant lady and women with children. It made me think of Jeremiah 31 and it was like a real sign from the Lord. We had four trips in June 1991 – 23rd, 25th, 27th and 29th – and then a break while the passport situations were sorted out; another bureaucratic joy!

The early days were times of great political upheaval, including a short but violent civil war in Moldova where we were sent to help evacuate Jewish people from the war zone. Due to the usual political and administrative difficulties, we were based in Odessa in the Ukraine. There we found a couple, Bob and Fi Doe, who had sailed across the Atlantic and were moored in Odessa. They had wanted to take Jewish people to Israel in the vessel. Such an initiative was not allowed by the Israeli government, so instead they provided a base for us. We stayed on their lovely yacht with running water, an absolute luxury, as there was no such thing in Odessa at that time. It was very comfortable, and seemed like the Lord's provision for us.

Domestic life in Eastern Europe could at best be described as rough and ready; the flats were very basic and there was often no electricity. If there was, it was generally delivered by a mass of bare electric wires that had no rhyme or reason for their directions! Water was frequently cut off for hours or days in some areas and altogether in others. Facilities for washing clothes and general housekeeping were real challenges. Everyday things in the West like washing powder, soap, deodorant, toothpaste, disinfectant, bleach and everything else in such categories were rare or non-existent. I shared a flat with Steve [Panchaud]. Neither of us were known to be really tidy. One day we were both in the office and our neighbour phoned. The flat door was open and, when they saw the mess, they thought we'd been burgled and phoned the police. We went home. The police were already there. Nothing had been stolen and the flat looked just like we'd left it! Working together as a team, despite the hassles, we could often see the funny side when we shared over a meal together at the end of the day.

As time has passed, and the number of olim helped is huge, I am pleased to relate that there have been great benefits for the Jewish people who made aliyah from the fSU. They enjoy a far higher standard of living. Being in the will of God has brought redemption, peace and hope to many, coming from non-belief to an understanding that God brought them back in faithfulness to his word. In a wider sense, it's not only a sign of God's faithfulness to the Jewish people; it is a sign to the Gentiles that God is working and is coming back soon (Isaiah 11:11-12).

The first field workers came from a variety of countries and often the girls drove the vehicles, from minibuses up to the massive Neoplan coaches as the work grew. There was a lot more to being a driver; it also required navigation and diplomatic skills as well as a working knowledge of basic mechanics and maintenance, which was part of everyday life. The Russian language was essential in the earliest days. One of the first workers was Ruth. Here is her story:

I first become aware of the *aliyah* movement while I was at university, possibly via James. I learned initially about the *refuseniks*, linked with the persecution of Christians. I subsequently went to a couple of prayer meetings and Bible Weeks where there was teaching by Intercessors for Britain, including one for young people, plus PWM (Prophetic Word Ministries) where Edmond Heddle, Jenny and David Forbes and Clifford Hill were speaking. I was also studying Russian.

After graduation I wanted to use my Russian in Christian work. I had contact with Pat when she worked in Holland and felt strongly that I was to go out and live in Russia. In March 1991 I decided I would stay on after a trip with Pat and then the opportunity opened up with Exobus. We heard about it from Steve Panchaud [the first Exobus worker] who subsequently came out to Moscow and from there we went on to the Ukraine.

We found ourselves in what might be termed virgin territory as no-one had tried this sort of thing before and there was no experience to draw from. Trying to work in an environment when there were obstacles at every step; breakdowns, freezing conditions and negotiations around border crossings were all part of daily life. Some of these pressures eased a bit when we had better relationships with the authorities in various areas, though we were still subject to the whims of the officials. One time, interpreting for co-worker Phil over border issues in Minsk, the official wanted to take us to a hunting lodge to wine and dine us, but Phil wouldn't go, saying something about being fed up with jumped-up petty officials getting in the way of things, which was fairly typical of him, but I had to interpret it a bit more tactfully.

In Moldova, there was an awful point when I was there with Ray and Viktor, two of our drivers. I was in the Cultural Centre in Tiraspol with some Israelis and I thought the guys were with the bus. Someone came in and asked if we were with the drivers and then said they had been arrested as agent provocateurs. They had been taking photos of the KGB offices. Along with one of the

Israelis and a photographer, Peter Gardner from the UK, we went to where they'd been told the guys had been taken, only to find that they had been moved. It turned out Viktor hadn't been arrested but had volunteered to go with Ray. Ari, the Israeli, was very anxious which meant I was also starting to get more anxious. After going through the office door, we were greeted by sandbags and a machine gun post!

To our relief we were told that they had been released. Unwittingly, as they had been sitting at a café, Ray had taken photos of a street scene, not realising the KGB building was in the shot. It was illegal in those days to take photographs of government buildings, railway stations, airports, shipping ports, military buildings, police stations and crossroads. It was all very tense and volatile. It even shocked Ray for a minute. Often the danger was more distant – you saw the odd body, heard gunfire – but this brought the reality of the situation closer. USA volunteer Debbie and I once stayed with a family in Zaparozhe. While they were out, the KGB paid a visit and basically said they were taking note of this event, causing some alarm for the locals.

Four trips had been planned for the first runs to Warsaw and the dates were set, but we didn't have any passengers. People simply didn't trust us. Steve went to a travel agent's location – office would be too strong a word – where the Jewish people could get tickets for the train to Warsaw. When he offered them the bus tickets, he got an aggressive response and nearly got beaten up. When he left, a few people followed him out and discreetly asked him for more information. A further tension was two-fold: the law relating to the age of conscription changed along with that for the renewal of passports. It meant that people had to leave suddenly (before the 1st of July); otherwise their passports would be cancelled and they would have to apply for new ones, meaning an indeterminate wait. But the timing was perfect from our point of view as it meant people were suddenly interested in the transport and services that we were offering.

A further positive move was when local believers started to work with us. This, however, was also initially a challenge and getting the locals on board had its own tensions. People were very suspicious of Westerners in general, or they expected us to have a lot of money. So I was excited when we gained their trust and they started to respond positively.

Once, whilst driving en-route to Korsten Shevchenko on the way to pick up olim on my own, the van broke down. It was a bit stressful because of the deadline to get them to the flight on time. I realised that it might be the filters, so I put on my overalls and started changing them. When I pulled my head out of the engine, there were a lot of people gathered around, and the men looked particularly shocked to see a Western girl doing this! But I got to the family okay and they were still packing! I met up with this family again when we were working in Israel; the man called me 'his angel'. We met many people in Israel that we had helped and it was good to see the full picture.

The following story is both funny and sad. We used to bring aid in the buses when we could and once brought in a busload of prosthetic limbs, unloading them into our office. One day James, Steve and I went for a drive in the country, something we very rarely did. We came across a broken-down vehicle and James and Steve offered their help. We got this couple to their dacha and had tea with them and got talking. The lady was the chief consultant for prosthetics for Afghan veterans; of course, we offered to help them with the prosthetics. She was happy and we delivered them to the hospital. All went well until she told her boss who refused the limbs because they were second-hand. We could see that the patients there had nothing in the way of prosthetics and the lady was very upset. She later phoned and asked if her patients could come to us. So they came to the office, picked out something and then arranged to have them fitted (and altered) themselves!

We lived as an international community in a cockroach-infested apartment, jokingly referred to as 'The Roach Motel.' I remember sitting in the hallway where we had our meals and hearing some faint unidentifiable music; it was cockroaches running up and down guitar strings! We went to the 'poison ladies' who said we had to evacuate the apartment, but it might take a while until they could do it. I went to visit them, but my contact lenses weren't working properly and my eyes were streaming. They took pity on me and dealt with the cockroaches effectively, but sad to say they were replaced by a huge rat!

Looking back at the countries we worked in, they were unstable politically and social corruption was rife. Our being there protected the Jewish people to a large degree as they travelled. Tough, thuggish border guards did seem to take advantage of the fact that people were leaving at every given opportunity on both sides of the borders.

From what we know, fewer Jewish people were coming from the former Soviet Union until the recent troubles in the Ukraine. There has also been a significant increase from other countries such as France and Belgium. Time moves on. People who had not thought of leaving before are now doing so due to different pressures. From my understanding of the Scriptures, aliyah will probably continue and increase as persecution rises in many different countries.

Flemming, who is from Denmark, was an early, much-valued field worker who received a baptism of fire upon moving into full-time aliyah-related ministry. Here is his story:

In 1986, after hearing Steve Lightle's vision on audio tape, I felt that I should help Jewish people when they come out of Russia via Scandinavia, especially through Denmark. At first I thought I'd help in Scandinavia and then realised I could help more immediately in Eastern Europe. For my last three years in education, I signed into a school where I could learn Russian. After school, I twice went on bus journeys (from Sweden and Finland) into Russia where we brought Jewish people back to Finland (from

St Petersburg). Both times we stayed in Finland, spending one day with the local Jewish people until they flew out to Israel. I was twenty at the time. Moses Hansen was involved in leading both these groups and he put me in touch with the Exobus project and sponsored me there for several years. So I came to England and joined Exobus in 1992.

The immediate post-Soviet republics encountered many challenges, not least in terms of governmental leadership and internal power struggles. Moldova descended into a vicious civil war. I joined Exobus in April and the conflict reached its peak some two months later. I remember being asked before every trip if we were willing to go in and whether we were aware of the dangers involved. I was driving a minibus and travelled with a guy from Israel who had war experience. It was sobering to see how tense he was going through checkpoints with drunken patrols who could be notoriously aggressive, demanding and trigger-happy. I wasn't really afraid because I knew I was in the right place at the right time. It was scary at times though. Whereas I did not see any direct fighting, the effects were all around; bullet holes, damaged buildings, craters, burnt-out tanks and equipment. What a contrast to staying on Bob and Fiona's yacht in Odessa where I remember racing their tortoises in the evenings!

Another major challenge was keeping the buses running in very cold temperatures. I remember getting up very early in the mornings to knock the vehicle free of ice. On one occasion in our garage compound in Kiev, the steering system completely froze, causing a great deal of damage. If that had happened on a passenger run, it would have been catastrophic. It would have been all but impossible to fix it in the frozen conditions at the roadside. The vehicle would have had to be recovered which would have taken a great deal of time, even if possible, and at unbelievable expense. In the event, it took us several days to repair.

I also recall driving all night (after driving through the day) to rescue another broken-down vehicle. The roads were very poor and full of potholes at the best of times, made worse by war-related damage. Police checks were frequent, challenging and very wearying. It was a constant battle to keep the buses in one piece as there were the on-going threats of broken axles, damaged wheels and broken suspensions. On one occasion I noticed smoke pouring out of the rear. Passengers weren't aware of anything, so I walked casually to the back of the bus to discover that the batteries were on fire! We ditched them, replaced them and calmly carried on; the passengers thankfully remained oblivious.

One of the most touching moments was in a small village. A Jewish man, on hearing that I was from Denmark, said it reminded him of when the Danish rescued Jews in World War II.

Flemming worked on the project for a good number of years – in Eastern Europe, mainland Europe and in the UK – and was a great encouragement to all. He now lives in Germany with his family.

To recap, buses had a driver and a courier. They were driven by young women as well as by young men and varied from minibuses to 40-plus seaters.

Judith is from Germany and was an early and long-time worker. She recalls some of her first experiences in 1993. Here is her story:

I first became aware of the aliyah movement in 1984. My father was part of the congregation Steve Lightle attended in Germany and shared what he had heard with the family. In 1992 I heard Christian Stephan of ICEJ Germany speak in Celle where I heard about the Exobus project. I also met members of the Exobus team at the ICEJ's Feast of Tabernacles in 1992 and subsequently joined the team the following year. I had started learning Russian in 1991 which was obviously God's preparation for what was to come. He had given me a word in 1988 from Isaiah 55:5, and in 1992 I realised he had been talking about the Jewish people.

I remember one time when our Mercedes van had engine problems. It kept stopping when it got hot. We were driving to

Krivoi Rog (about eight hours) and the engine stopped when we arrived, but we got to the family we were picking up okay. We set off and after a short time the engine again started having problems. I changed the filters, but that didn't help. I remembered the story of the king who went ahead of the army singing praises. So I started to quietly sing praise songs to the Lord. When I sang, the engine would go; if I stopped, the engine would stop! The passengers, worried about the condition of the van, asked to be dropped at the next railway station. But when we got there everything was fine, so they carried on. I sang for over five hours! Finally, about 50 km before the airport, we were rescued by one of our other vehicles. The head of the family hugged me at the end of the journey, saying: 'God brought us here'.

On one occasion, early in my time in the Ukraine, I picked up a young family with a small baby in the middle of winter. I don't remember the place, but I was to discover for the first time that it was a typical out-of-city town. Typically, they only had water and heating for a few hours each day, and the condition of the buildings and sanitary facilities was appalling. The toilets were outside with no flush mechanisms and would freeze in the winter. Food supplies were very scarce and of poor quality. It was so good to know that the baby was getting out of that awful situation.

When we were working in Kharkov, we developed a close relationship with the Israel-Jewish Cultural Centre there. They had some girls from the IDF come over for a few months to teach Hebrew, Jewish culture and traditions. They found life in the Ukraine quite challenging, especially in the hygiene department, and would even boil lettuce to make sure it was safe to eat. They also asked us a lot of questions about why we were there and one said, 'We are jealous of you because you know God better than we do.' Praise the Lord!

Flemming and Judith married and continued to work on the project for a good number of years. They now are involved in the

Ezra work in Germany. Daniella, from Bulgaria, was also part of the international team. Here is her story:

I first became aware of the *aliyah* movement when I was at Bible School in Sweden. I was involved in a prayer group there for Israel. I visited the Mary Sisters at Darmstadt, Germany, and heard Phil Hunter speak. After the meeting I asked him for some brochures and told him I came from Bulgaria. He asked if I spoke Russian, saying that this was an important skill needed for the work. It was 1992.

After I finished Bible School, I contacted the Exobus office in Hull. Via the ICEJ in Germany, I went to Warsaw and then on to Kiev to join the team. An unforgettable experience was my first trip from Dnepropetrovsk to Kiev, seeing things come alive and seeing the people waiting with all their luggage (then only two bags per person). The whole process was something remarkable; emotional, exciting and challenging all at the same time.

One of the biggest challenges we faced concerned the security of the passengers, their documents and money, luggage and the vehicles. The first years of the post-Communist era were lawless in many parts of the Ukraine and banditry was rife. I always felt on tenterhooks. We had a scary situation involving three minibuses en-route to Chernigov, to help with Aliyah, when a bus broke down. So we changed stuff around in a car park and were almost immediately aware that we were being watched. When we got on the road again, some vehicles followed us and tried to make us stop. We managed to lose them in Kiev, but they had chased us for about two hours.

Communications were another challenge. We had no phone in the house in Kharkov and had to go to the Post Office (this was before mobiles) to phone. We made all the arrangements for 'runs' via the PO phone! It always made you feel very vulnerable. I don't know how we organised everything without a phone! God's grace was sufficient!

A constant problem was that it could be very hard to start the vehicles at the commencement of a journey, particularly early in the morning, and keep them going. If the engine cut out for any reason, the cold made it a nightmare to get it up and running again. Clearing frozen glass, and keeping it clear along with frozen locks, were all part of the daily routine through the long and dark winter months. Once the bus broke down and ended up in a ditch. It was minus 20 degrees centigrade and there were no auto clubs or rescue services, no roadside emergency phones, so you can imagine the difficulties.

All these years later, it is good to look back and reflect upon the fact that the people we helped had lived in a land where they were disadvantaged and not fully accepted. We helped to provide them with a chance to express their own identity and feel understood in addition to enjoying a better standard of living.

Chapter 9

Indigenous Workers

One of the biggest changes over the years of Christian-sponsored aliyah is that of the position of the local believers who were involved. In the very early days, as with all the organisations on the field, the majority of the workers – and certainly the leaders – were Western volunteers. Over the years this gradually changed to the extent that now, on the field, almost all the workers are local believers and nearly all the leadership positions are also now held by local believers.

At the very beginning with Good News (and this was true for others too), Ukrainian law demanded that these Western organisations were under the umbrella of a Ukrainian entity. But this changed within a couple of years. Natasha Golik, sadly no longer with us, was the liaison person with the company under which Good News initially operated. She was not at first a believer but was really a kind of 'spy' within the organisation. However, she was very impressed by the Westerners then working for Good News/Exobus in the Ukraine – Debbie from America, Steve, Ruth and James from the UK and Sib from Holland. She was most curious when they were in the office behind closed doors having prayer times and Bible studies. After a fairly short period, Natasha gave her life to the Lord and served him faithfully from that time onwards. She was the first point of contact in Kiev for the thousands of Jewish people and helped with transport from their homes to the airport. Because of the poor phone connections, she could be heard constantly shouting information into the phone to those asking for help. She patiently answered questions that were asked over and over again. She also served as 'courier' on the buses – drivers took care of the driving and vehicle, of course, and practical aspects of the journey, and the couriers took care of the passengers. Natasha's genuine love and concern for people broke through many barriers. One story that she was fond to relate took place on a journey from Chernovtsy in Western Ukraine to Kiev. She had travelled there in the coach the day before along with the two Finnish drivers, Hannu and Mika. The journey back to Kiev airport took around 14 hours so they had to be ready quite early in the morning at the departure point. One Jewish family was late and there was some debate as to how long they could wait without risking being late for the flight. Finally, they turned up and boarded the bus.

As always on the journey, once the people had settled down, the courier would give a short speech on the practical points to follow. A little later, another short speech would be given on how the team represented Christians from all over the world, who love Israel and the Jewish people, while also sharing some Scriptures on the re-gathering of the Jews. Natasha always said that the atmosphere in the buses always got 'colder' when the word Christian was mentioned. On this day, the man of the family who arrived late shouted out, 'You Christians; you've stolen our God.' Natasha lifted her voice in silent prayer asking for wisdom and then answered, 'Well, sir, you may be right. But we – Hannu, Mika and I – are ready to give him back to you. Are you ready to receive him?' By the end of the journey the man had completely changed his attitude, hugging Natasha goodbye at the airport, full of thanks. He had seen and felt practical Christian love in action.

Natasha would often say laughingly in the office, 'We have had another miraculous healing today!' Very often, when families phoned, they would say they had an elderly family member who found it difficult to walk and needed a 'lying' place in the vehicle. But often the extent of the disability was exaggerated and, when the family was picked up, it was discovered that, while there was some level of problem, a 'lying' place was not really needed; hence Natasha's 'miraculous healings'.

Natasha's wisdom and love of people won over many Jewish hearts, but she was also the mother of the Good News team, listening to everyone's problems, dispensing wisdom and good common sense as she could. Although she became vice-president of the charity in the Ukraine, she always described herself as 'Helper of the Helpers'.

She had a wonderfully dry sense of humour and sometimes you were not quite sure. In the office in Podol, Kiev, the team used to lunch together. Food supplies were quite difficult and meat was hard to get hold of. On one occasion, whilst there on a teaching and training exercise, I entered the office to the delicious smell of meat stew. Whilst we were enjoying it, I asked what was in it. 'Rabbit' she replied. 'It was my pet; it died this morning!'

Natasha finally retired in the summer of 2008. She had been helping an elderly Jewish lady for some time named Ida, who was very much on her own and the help the team gave her ranged from taking her to hospital appointments and selling her belongings as well as the normal aliyah-related help. Although Natasha decided to retire, she made a commitment to continue helping Ida until she made her aliyah. Not long after retirement, Natasha became seriously ill and went to be with her Lord on Christmas Eve 2008, the day after Ida flew out to Israel!

Natasha, of course, was not the only Ukrainian believer to play a significant role. Initially all the Good News drivers were Western, apart from Wiktor from Poland. Wiktor was a great asset to the team not just because of his driving but also because of his ability to speak Russian and help solve some of the practical problems. In the first few years, all the vehicles were right-hand drive, but that changed with the acquisition of left-hand drive British ex-army vehicles from Germany known as the Sons of Jacob! Several local believers had already been driving smaller vehicles. The first one was Andrei Dzonyak who, though no longer working full-time for aliyah, continues to help with driving olim to Kiev airport to this day. With the arrival of the Sons of Jacob, gradually more and more of the drivers were local rather than Western. The changing laws made it increasingly difficult to continue using Western drivers and became another source of contention with the traffic police. Outside of Kiev the bases soon began to be totally run and led by local team members. One of the consequences of this was a change from the main team language being English to Russian. Natasha from Belarus joined the Good News team in 1997, initially for six months, and eventually led the base in Dnepropetrovsk, the second biggest of all the bases. Natasha is still working in Aliyah, serving with Ezra. There are too many key people to name them all, and relate their stories, but without them it is questionable whether the work could have continued in the way that it has.

While Ebenezer was running the ship, there was also a high involvement of Western volunteers who were able to go and serve for a minimum of three months. After the sailings were finished, the involvement of Westerners continued, but to a lesser degree. It was still possible to volunteer and go on 'fishing' trips in the Ukraine alongside some of the local believers. As time went on, leadership within the countries also passed to local believers.

Perhaps due to starting a few years later when the situation had already changed, Ezra has had less involvement from Western volunteers over the years. At the very beginning, a Scandinavian couple were involved in getting things established and, over the years, various volunteers lived and worked in Kiev for differing lengths of time. Within a relatively short period, a young local believer took over the leadership and saw Ezra's work expand from Ukraine into many of the other fSU countries. He still leads Ezra's work in Ukraine today, along with several other responsibilities. All the workers on the field in the former Soviet Union today are local believers, some from very supporting churches.

The move to local believers being responsible is very important. Helping the Jewish people in any given country is largely the responsibility of the church there, giving the work an authentic contour. In some places that is not possible, and in some others there remains the need for outside help, particularly in starting things up. Apart from the spiritual dynamic, there are also practical benefits; they know the language and understand the culture!

Currently the bulk of across-the-board finance for aliyah continues to come from the West. However, local churches in many of the fSU countries are now contributing financially. There is also considerable prayer support. Not long ago Ezra's team in Irkutsk, Siberia, which is part of a local Word of Life church, sent a gift to help with the situation in Eastern Ukraine. Undoubtedly, this was sacrificially given. There are also a number of pastors among the volunteers, sometimes using church or personal vehicles to bring olim to the airports.

Along with their practical help in all sorts of ways, many local believers from across all the ministries are also involved in networking, speaking with local pastors, preaching in churches, taking tours to Israel from Ukraine, Russia, Moldova and Uzbekistan and Kazakhstan! Ezra's director in Moldova is the pastor of a small church, specifically formed with support of Israel at its core. Igor was recently named 'Man of the Year' by the local Jewish organisations in Kishinev because of his work in aliyah.

Misha is one of the longest-serving Ukrainian nationals who worked both with GNT and Ezra. Here is his story:

I first became aware of the Lord's plan for the Jewish people whilst a student at the Word of Life Bible School in Estonia. An element of the teaching programme focused on aliyah. Whereas I thought this was a new but relevant thing, I didn't think it applied to me at the time. After Bible School I read an uncensored version of Anatoly Kuznetsov's book on Babi Yar; it made a deep and lasting impression on me. At this time, I worked in the Podol area of Kiev where the Exobus buses were based, more commonly known as Good News Travels. I often wondered about them: what they were and what they were about. Western organisations were rare at the time. Later, in February 1994, there was a group in Kiev from Word of Life Sweden and through them I was introduced to Sib, GNT's representative, by a friend, Sasha, who worked with them in aliyah. He had made aliyah himself some time previously and was back to work such projects. He suggested that I should apply to work with GNT as a courier. I was very excited by this opportunity which led to an interview with Sib. When he interviewed me, the language employed was English. Sadly, I knew very little English at the time, so Sib said 'no'. I was devastated. My heart's desire was to do something to help the Jewish people, especially with their return. The Maim Chaim dance group had started by then and I was blessed to be taken on part-time to help with the moving and setting up of equipment and ironing costumes! This was summer '94. I gladly did that for several months. Sib saw my desire and allowed me to start as a courier with drivers who spoke a little Russian. I bought myself a phrase book and started to learn English. On my first time as a courier the 'run' lasted three days! I was there assisting another courier and, as I observed the work, not only did I feel it was the Lord's word in action; I felt deeply this was the Lord's calling for me.

The first run with the olim was very emotional, especially seeing people saying goodbye to their families and friends. None of them knew whether they would ever see each other again. At first it was very hard to speak to them as the bus pulled away. Before every run I would feel an overwhelming sense of responsibility for the people as we went to the airport. Finding the words and way to speak to them at the beginning was a challenge, but by the end of a run we had become family.

An overwhelming sense of freedom for them and the knowledge that we had done our part in God's plan brought a great sense of joy as we departed on our way back from the airport. We were also filled with the anticipation of how the Lord would use us in his next challenging assignment.

If and when the bus broke down, which was not unusual, it was very challenging in those days. Initially, there were no mobile phones and, once we had them, there were very few places with a good enough signal. We really had to rely on God's help. On one occasion when a bus 'died on us', I hitched a ride on a motorbike to the nearest village where there was only one telephone. As was usual in those days, telephones only worked when the electricity was working, and the electricity was down. I was very concerned as I had a full bus of olim. When the electricity supply was restored, I was finally able to phone our office in Kiev. By God's grace, another bus had just unloaded at the airport and was able to rescue us; we were about an hour's drive away. Praise God we made it on time despite all of this!

On one run from East Ukraine a man in his mid-40s came to me and said: "A stone has fallen from my heart because I see that someone loves us!" He had experienced a lot of anti-Semitism in his life and our service to him on this run touched him deeply.

Anti-Semitism is, sadly, widespread in Ukraine. One year I took my grandmother some matza. She wouldn't eat it because she said it was made by Jews who mixed it with Christian blood.

My local church and its pastor in Kiev didn't support this ministry even though several people from the church were involved. He was in one sense afraid that working with the Jewish people could cause severe problems.

Misha's testimony sadly rings true. A large church in Kiev supported the idea of aliyah in the early days. As the congregation grew rapidly to around 2,000-plus people, the leader was moved to hold a service of repentance and reconciliation at Babi Yar. The site is a ravine on the outskirts of Kiev where Einsazgruppen units of the SS and local nationalists massacred 33,771 Jews within just two days in September 1941. A visit from the local authorities soon put paid to the idea with the threat of closing the church if such an event took place. Since that point in the early 1990s, Israel and aliyah were seldom mentioned until recently.

A most effective way of reaching Jewish communities, and also of gaining access to churches, was with our dance and drama team. Many of the contacts were given to us by the Jewish Agency, or just by visiting Jewish areas and knocking on doors. An important aspect of the door-knocking was to take gifts of food and toiletries as there were drastic shortages almost everywhere.

A rep's life is a very busy one; here is an extract from the diary of an Ezra rep in the eastern Ukraine during the recent troubles in the Donbas region. The following is not untypical!

On 7 April [2015] I got up at 01:00 and collected eight people from the base outside Dnepropetrovsk and took them to the airport. Then I went to another base and picked up a family from there and took them to the airport. Home at 19:30. On 8 April: I went to the base to pick up nine people and took them to the airport. I sent these people off and took another two people to the bus station. Then I went to the other base and took a family of five to the consul. I also met another family to organise their foreign passports. Home at 22:30. On 9 & 10 April: Various meetings. On 14 April: Travel to pick up families from Mariupol to take them to their consular check. I left at 07:00 and returned at 18:00.

Today the work continues apace and local believers work as hard as ever. The work in the Ukraine has become increasingly difficult following the Russian annexations. Drivers have been arrested on no real charges and a multitude of militias are forever demanding any number of things! Corruption abounds and red tape is everywhere.

Chapter 10

Family Matters

As the narrator I expect that I should share some of our own family experiences in a more detailed way. My desire is to honour the Lord's extraordinary way of using ordinary people to do the most extraordinary things for the purposes of His kingdom and the sanctification of His holy name (Ezekiel 36:16f). My own testimony is scattered throughout the book, but it may be worth adding a couple of incidents that confirmed the calling to work with the Jewish people.

Shortly after we first realised the Lord's calling and purposes for the Jewish people, I was at a 6am prayer meeting when I had a vision of a Russian train. In those days they had massive trains and they flew flags on either side of the front of the locomotive. When they arrived at railway stations, they would be greeted by loud patriotic music accompanied by choirs. The vision was of a large train pulling into a snow-covered station; the people who were getting off were Jewish and reaching out their hands. As burly guards stood in between them and me, I felt a deep compassion and the Lord said, 'You are needed.' I also felt a call to visit Budapest and Odessa.

A few weeks later came our monthly town-wide prayer meeting, but it was also my day off. Life had been very hectic at the school and the church. We were in Peterborough where we had taken one of our sons for a job interview. There were no mobile phones, but I had a primitive 'bleep'. When the device went off, you phoned your office. It duly bleeped and when I got through to my PA, I was told that one of the other pastors who should have taken the meeting was ill and the other one was in Wales. Could I please take the meeting? The guests that night were missionaries who were serving in China under the guise of English language teachers. So I rather grudgingly rushed the hundred or so miles back to Colchester and got there just in time for the worship session. The man then spoke of their work and I felt very warm towards the couple whose testimony was compelling and encouraging. The lady then got up and said, nervously, that she had something to share. She said she had never shared this before, but it was vision that the Lord had given her. It was the same vision the Lord had given others concerning aliyah including my wife Maria. So I got up and said that as a church this was a core value. The man then asked to share a word, which I assumed would be for the church. However, he started to sing in the spirit. I felt the power of the Lord over me in an unusual way, and he then delivered this word to me: "You have been chosen for a special ministry, to a special people, the Jewish people. You will never ask to be involved; you will be sent for, and many will come to you." Needless to say, I felt completely overwhelmed. The rest is history!

In terms of history, it seems right to start with the testimony of my long-suffering wife and partner in ministry, Maria:

I grew up in a wonderful Bible-based family. As a young girl my grandfather would teach me the parables and a wonderful array of Bible stories. In common with many Christians, I knew that there existed a modern-day State of Israel and that Jesus was Jewish. However, I probably never gave it a second thought! All of which was to change dramatically during a time of prayer while at the Elim Bible College in the early 1980s. The college was then situated in a beautiful old building surrounded by landscaped grounds in Capel, Surrey. We were preparing for a life in pastoral ministry within the movement. We felt at home there and enjoyed good relationships with the leadership and were set to take the unusual step of pioneering a new church.

But our future and calling was to be very different. The Lord showed me a strange and deeply disturbing but fascinating picture. Before me was a highly-elevated roadway that many people were desperately attempting to clamber upon. They were of all ages, sizes, ethnicity and physical descriptions. Some were blind, some were lame and some were pregnant. They seemed in the main to be desperate and impoverished and were carrying their scant possessions in their hands. Some were even holding their hearts in their hands and walking bowed over with tears in their eyes. As they were trying to access the road, they were being assisted by people who were offering both physical and practical help. At the end of their journey stood the Lord with his arms outstretched.

Shortly afterwards, Fred graduated and became pastor of a church plant in Colchester – quite an innovative idea at the time! While we were establishing it, we met with an American missionary. After coffee and conversation, we began a time of prayer together. I felt strangely prompted by the Spirit to share this vision with him but held back as there seemed no obvious reason to do so. I was not in the least bit confident to share things like this, particularly with other people. However, feeling compelled, I did so with some trepidation. At once he started to weep; my first thought was that in some way I had either upset or offended him. He proceeded to tell me that others had had similar dreams and visions. The Lord was and still is calling Christians to help the Jewish people return to their ancient homeland in fulfilment of the prophetic scriptures, especially Isaiah 49:22. I immediately felt as if a bright spiritual light had been switched on and was illuminating something dynamic and deeply challenging. I was overwhelmed by the enormity of the revelation.

He proceeded to share scriptures from the major prophets and we sat in something like a state of shock and awe. We both knew from that moment that the Lord had spoken to us and that this would be our calling from then on; impossible as it seemed.

Following this ground-breaking position, we immediately got in touch with the late Ken Burnett at Prayer for Israel and in a very short space of time met Steve Lightle, whose book *Exodus II* was shedding renewed focus on what we now term aliyah. It is probably fair to say that from good hearts and enthusiasm for what the Lord had shown us, we almost expected to be immediately involved in full-blown aliyah. But it was some time before it became a reality. Looking back, maybe that is what was needed then. A lot of Steve's message was about the state of the heart, which sadly got lost in a sense of the excitement of what seemed far in the distant future.

But eventually things moved at breakneck speed and within no time our church situation changed. We amalgamated with another local fellowship and there was an immediate focus on Israel. We had soon established a PFI prayer group and had visits from people who were to become leaders of the proto-aliyah movement whom we featured at our monthly town-wide prayer meetings.

Wonderful evenings were spent in our home with Kjell Sjoberg, Johannes Fascius, Eliyahu Ben-Haim, David Forbes, Lance Lambert, Gerald Gotzen and others. Kjell asked Fred to do research for him and then speak with him on teaching tours while David encouraged him to write articles for academic journals as well as books.

One winter in the middle 1980s the late Johannes was staying with us to undertake a number of meetings including praying and planning for Siberia. Ironically, we were completely snowed in! I asked him what the Lord required of an intercessor within this most important ministry. I will never forget his response. This may not be quite how he put it, but it was gracious, gentle, kind and reassuring: "Don't do prayer. Let your life become a constant prayer!"

He spent the next three days watching movies and eating sweets in the morning with our youngest son, Daniel. (The last time I saw Johannes, shortly before he died, he still regarded Dan as his friend.) Later, he was up until the early hours poring over Bible texts and seeking the Lord to try and gain some understanding of how to progress. I remember Johannes had something akin to an early version of what would become a mobile phone – a huge briefcase with another one for the battery! We thought it was futuristic!

Almost at once during that first summer we began to undertake prayer journeys into Eastern Europe where we interceded for the captive Jewish people at strategic points. Many times we walked along the Berlin Wall asking that it would fall and that the Jewish people would stream out alongside many others. I remember a particular piece of graffiti that proclaimed 'Jesus can walk through this wall!' This was to become a reality. Despite the first truck that entered the former East Germany through Checkpoint Charlie being full of pornographic literature, the churches grew at an unprecedented rate.

It is a little-known fact that the remnant of believers in East Germany played an essential role in the collapse of the USSR dominance. While we were there, we met a senior pastor from Leipzig and were enthralled when he told us that the remnant church there were praying daily, repenting of the Holocaust and asking the Lord not only to bring down the Wall but also to return the Jewish people to Israel. The prayer gathering increased to thousands and torchlight processions took place on Fridays. Despite their attempts to quell the meetings, the authorities eventually gave way, which pulled the trigger for freedom!

A couple of nights before the 'trigger', we were on the Polish–German border on our way home after a long and arduous journey. We had slept in the van the previous night after a very early start and had been unable to get any decent food. The crossing was one of the least used and usually took just a couple of hours to get through. When we got there, we were pleased to see that there was nothing in front of us, but they did not beckon us forward. Two or three hours passed. We weren't particularly perturbed as sometimes you would have to wait several hours for no good reason. We always listened to the BBC World Service on the radio to try and keep us up to date. To our amazement, the newscaster began to tell the story of the mass breakouts in Hungary. We rejoiced that our prayers against the monolith of Communism might start to be answered, little expecting what came next. Suddenly there was a flurry of activity, all of the big spotlights being switched on and car sirens sounding, their lights flashing. The guards seemed agitated and rushed around loading their weapons. But just as quickly as it started, some ten minutes later the situation suddenly quietened and the guards walked back to their posts. An hour later we were still sitting in the quiet in what seemed an empty space. Suddenly the guards simply lifted the barrier and walked away; the last one just waved us forward in a resigned manner and all the lights went out, leaving total darkness.

Tentatively, we started to drive forward. There were no guards or the usual security measures. The several barriers, traffic lights, offices and vehicle inspection bays were all empty, along with anything else which might have impeded our progress. All of the many arc lights were turned off and there were no signs of soldiers or guards. It was silent and quite eerie. Not quite sure of what was going on, we were very alert to any possibility of unexperienced dangers and drove through East Germany without incident or any further news.

When we got to the West German border at daybreak, we still had to go through the usual protocols, but one of the guards said something along the lines of, 'How on earth did you get through tonight?' We told him the story and he looked slightly perplexed.

After such a long journey, along with the strange events and lack of substantial food for two days, we were pleased to reach the first food stop. It seemed so clean compared with the previous few weeks. Even though it was early morning, my friend Roy ordered a steak for two people. When it arrived, he humorously declared, 'Gee, I don't know whether to eat this or worship it!' This was when we got the news that East Germany had fallen.

In these pre-aliyah years it also seemed that everywhere we travelled we would meet Jewish people from the USA or Eastern Europe who were visiting places where their families had lived before being destroyed in the Holocaust. They were wonderful times and some kept contact, especially one family from Firenze we met in Berlin.

Travel in Eastern Europe was very different in those days. You could only drive on roads that had yellow stripes on the sides. Stray off them and you would immediately be arrested. The roads were also screened by tall pine trees so that you could not see anything at all on either side. If you came to a crossroads, you were stopped and questioned, and some sort of gratuity was expected. Many big cities outside of the capitals only had one hotel. By the time you got a visa, they were generally booked for months in advance! Often the only option was to sleep in the van.

Sometimes we lived for days on end in the back of the van or vans with which the Lord blessed us for our travel. We moved from city to city, town to town, and through numerous schtetels, travelling over 5,500 miles on one occasion. On occasions we stayed in what might best be described as 'Cockroach Hotels' – five-star being the highest number of cockroaches keeping you company down to one star for the least, but even that would not be tolerated in the West!

On one two instances, by the Lord's grace, we ended up in the presidential or bridal suites. Ironically enough, these magnificent but fading edifices of pre-Communist rule cost less to stay in than the cheaper concrete non-entity alternatives nearby. Whenever you stayed in a hotel in those days, there were always internal security agents watching you. A humorous aside was in Kluj, Romania, where they had agents in the hotel lobby who sat there in case any Westerners arrived. Fred struck up a relationship with the manager who pointed out who the two men assigned to us were. He approached them, told them that we were tourists and said, 'Don't bother following us; join us for dinner and show us around.' But they weren't allowed to do that. Still, we bought them a good dinner to be taken in the lobby and team members later shared a drink with them, subtly asking where the Jewish people were before turning in. On the way back, we stayed in the same hotel and renewed our acquaintance.

I have been asked on several occasions what is the most outstanding memory of the blessings of this time. Maybe one of the most overwhelming times was our second visit to Romania. Our church had sent out a married couple as a forward movement to Isai, where the Iron Guard (Legion of the Archangel Michael) was founded. Under the Nazi occupation, the Iron Guard murdered at least 65,000 Jewish people in Odessa (Ukraine) during the war by burning them alive or blowing them up in warehouses as the preferred method! We pulled up unannounced outside the synagogue in Isai and the couple who looked after it came out with some measure of trepidation. As I got out, the lady rushed towards me with tears in her eyes. She said she had been waiting for this visit after seeing me in her dreams and had prayed for many years for this to happen. In view of all that had happened, she could not believe that anyone cared enough about them to visit them. It was both humbling and overwhelming.

They took us round their synagogue, one of the last remaining out of 28 before the outbreak of hostilities. There were few artefacts left, but they were treasured and showed with pride and pathos. Our youngest son Daniel, then only ten and wearing a kippah as a sign of respect, took it off as we left and gave it to the keeper, who didn't even have a paper one. The dear elderly man took it in his hands and wept profusely. In all his adult life, he had never had one! It may seem strange these days, but when you think about it, it is not that long ago. Under Communism, any external signs of Judaism were proscribed.

Most people might not appreciate this but, in the 1980s when Communism was an Iron Wall, Christian presence was negligible in Eastern Europe and the number of Christians supporting Israel was, shall we say, so low that we knew nearly all who were involved!

East Germany was a place we visited often while it was still under Communism. It was always a challenge crossing the borders as the guards were the worst of any in Eastern Europe in terms of delays, over-searching and demanding bribes. We had found a network of Lutheran churches where the congregations were often in single figures, but the pastors, surprisingly, had a heart for Israel and the Jewish people. We found a point of access through education and cultural exchanges via the school. We had many wonderful encounters there with Jewish people who were fleeing the fSU helped by these dear ones including some who had deserted the Soviet Army.

One day at the pastor's house near Magdeburg where we were staying, there was a knock on the door. We opened it to be confronted by two Russian soldiers. Rather than investigating why we were there, they were begging for food. We invited them in, gave them something to eat and a warm drink, and they told us their story. They had been stationed nearby for just over two years. They had not been paid for months and were regularly beaten by their officers because they were Jewish and regarded as useless mouths to feed. In common with some of the other soldiers, they had sold pieces of their kit simply to eat and looked pale and ragged.

After we had fed them and tried to find out anything that might be useful for them, they told us of a group of Jewish people who were under a form of arrest at a nearby tractor factory. They were living on starvation rations. We immediately set out to find them. To my surprise, the Lord had shown me the location a few days previously in a dream about the Jewish people. We gained entry to the site and were met with great suspicion. The leader of the group, Aleksander, was an ex-officer in the Diplomatic Unit of the Soviet Army where he had worked as a translator. He explained that the forty-plus who were there had all attempted to leave the USSR via Germany, had been apprehended, and were about to be sent back – in his case, to Odessa – where they would face criminal charges.

The situation had been exacerbated by the fact that they only had tea and one sandwich a day to live on, plus five ostmarks a day (virtually no value), and a family room measuring seven feet by five. The sanitary conditions were poor and there were no real laundry or bathing facilities. An enterprising pair of brothers launched a failed plan to help. Valery and Mischa, who we affectionately nick-named 'the blues brothers', launched a scheme to buy arms and munitions from the starving soldiers to sell on the black market. They had been caught and were now in prison, but the whole group were facing criminal charges on arrival back in the USSR.

We immediately left and bought up as much food and water as we could to take back to them. They were overwhelmed, which gave us the opportunity to tell them who we were and why we were there – all of which was met with great surprise.

We also shared the scriptures about their own identity and their destiny in the land and how we were called and worked to facilitate it. In this instance, being able to help these dear ones seemed outside of reasonable possibility. But as usual 'instant mouth' kicked in and we said we would see what we could do to help.

We returned to where we were staying and related the story to Andreas, the pastor, and a friend of his. He said the only way anything could be done was to approach the provincial governor. His friend knew someone who worked in the office. We prayed about it as a team and made the decision that Fred, Bernhart, our translator, and George, the pastor's friend, would go and see said official, stupid and dangerous as it sounded.

That evening we were due to take a house meeting for members of the four local churches. As Fred and Bernhart were away, it fell to me to lead it. So far, so good, but I did not speak German and nobody there spoke English! We started with a prayer and Bible reading and, to my utter amazement, the Holy Spirit enabled me to take the meeting in German! God's grace and provision never ceases to bless me.

When I look back over these many years, I remember well when Fred said to me in the late 1990s, 'We have helped the Jewish people return for many years, but what about those that can't?' It was at the turn of the century when indirect absorption halted and the situation for some was going to change. In simple terms this meant that those who did not have relatives or were too sick, in debt or could not obtain various permissions could not leave. How could we do this! Our first thought was to locate those with whom we had previously worked and see if they could help. We had no idea what to do.

I remember well meeting with members of the old team and a few new people who were friends of theirs in Kiev. It seemed extremely strange to be exploring an element of ministry that we would not even have considered before.

In the eighties and early nineties, there was great anticipation that, when the Soviet empire fell, we would see the big exodus prophesied in the Bible. Aliyah has been a wonderful series of events and testimonies, but it could reasonably be said we were still awaiting something of greater magnitude. All I can say is that I do not think the church is in a right place today, largely because of anti-Semitism, to be prepared for their call and destiny for this end-time event. Having said that, the end-times are 'triggered' by the 'Banner to the Nations' (Isa 11:11-12) – namely, the return of the Jewish people to their covenanted land and their destiny in Messiah.

I feel absolutely blessed to have been allowed to play a small part in the momentous events we have witnessed, some of which we have shared here. The miracle that God uses ordinary, everyday people to help bring about the return to the land of the Jewish people and their reconciliation with Him to fulfil their destiny, is both challenging and, at times, overwhelming. Surely it is one of the greatest of privileges.

I will now pick up where Maria left off concerning the visit to the provincial governor. We first became involved in East Germany in 1987 when communism had an iron grip on the country. We had established contact with a group of Lutheran churches who had a heart for repentance for Nazi Germany and their treatment of the Jews. Under communism, pastors were allowed to attend seminary for training, but on graduation and appointment, generally to a group of churches, they would have to report to the local police and Stasi who, after beating and bullying them, made them pledge not to evangelise – not that there were many opportunities.

The group we were with consisted of three pastors with around twelve churches to look after with very small congregations, Nazi memorial plaques around the balcony and a huge pulpit surrounded by two enormous white marble angels. It was a strange sensation speaking about aliyah in these surroundings, but the message was met with great enthusiasm and a special meeting convened for prayer and repentance.

Following the meeting with the Russian soldiers, we got the address and proceeded to see what could be done to help. We arrived at the factory and the guard was happy to receive us in exchange for a couple of pens. We found a group of around thirty men, women and a couple of children and were met by Sasha, an ex-army captain who had become leader of the group. We immediately toured the four churches along with friends of the pastors to organise a daily food run. In the midst of the flurry of activity, two young men, Misha and Valery, were arrested for selling Russian army rifles to buy food for the hungry soldiers.

When asked where they were hoping to go, most said America but some wanted to enter West Germany; only two were interested in going to Israel. We had a long discussion around the scriptures and a significant number said on reflection that Israel might be a better option. We said we'd see what we could do. For what on reflection some 32 years later can only be described as a direct word from the Lord or plain insanity, the decision was made to approach the provincial governor on their behalf. We were assisted by Bernhart, a German-born young man from our church who came as translator, and an English-speaking member of one of the congregations who was a petty government official.

To our surprise, when we arrived at the building, without being asked our business, we were informed we would be seen if we cared to wait. About twenty minutes later the door opened and a slightly built man wearing a fur trimmed coat and trilby hat entered the room accompanied by two enormous bodyguards. All of them were smoking the customary cigarette at the prescribed angle. He introduced himself as the provincial governor and asked the nature of our business. He listened with a blank face and dismissed the bodyguards with a wave, ordered tea over the intercom and asked me a few personal questions. He paced around the room chain-smoking and, when the tea arrived, dismissed his secretary from the adjoining office. He asked why we wanted to help Jews. I explained the scriptural remit and he said: 'I know all about the Bible.' It turned out he was Jewish! I could hardly believe my ears. He went on, 'My father survived the Shoah by pretending to be Catholic and served as submariner in Kreigsmarine during the war. He is still alive and leads a small unofficial Jewish community here in Magdeburg.' He proceeded to say that he was aware of the group of people we were discussing. The problem, he explained, was that their presence and behaviour was causing problems for their small unofficial community.

A pause and cigarette later, he shrugged his shoulder and said he was sympathetic but had no idea what could be done. I asked him if he believed in the God of Abraham, Isaac and Jacob, to which he replied in the affirmative. I asked him if believed in prayer; he did. I read him the passage where Moses' hands were lifted, and put it to him, 'Could we lift up his arms and pray for him?' to which, to our further surprise, he readily agreed. Finally, he asked if we had any transport and would the Jewish Agency have papers and so on for these if they could get to Tegel Airport after which they would be free to cross to a third party Western country. If so, he said there would be no police or officials on the route between midnight and 2am the following day. He took the pastor's number and said he would be in touch by ten that evening. We left in a state of shock, to say the least. Around 9.30 there was a call from Berlin where he had gone immediately after we had left. He said he had been able to cancel all the charges and deportation orders and would quietly arrange facilities for those who wanted to stay or those who wanted to leave and they would get the correct papers very quickly.

In the event, the single young men went to Israel almost immediately while some with children went to West Germany and a few to the USA. Sasha, the leader of the group, initially went to Geissen in West Germany where we kept in contact with him for a number of years. He kept us abreast of what happened to those who went to Israel.

We were very soon introduced to a pastor from Leipzig who was in some senses a spiritual father to them. He had a great passion for the reunification of Germany and an end to communism. In addition, he had a huge heart for the Jewish people and their return to the land, of whom there were a significant number of both Germans and Russians in East Germany. He told us he was one of the leaders of the Peace Prayer movement in Leipzig and also led a group praying for repentance for the Shoah. It was one of the most staggering hidden Christian initiatives I have ever encountered, and we were soon to appreciate the power of their prayer.

The prayer initiative commenced in Nicolaikirche (St Nicholas Church) built in 1165 in the inner city of Leipzig. From the 1970s, there was no venue to gather and discuss anything outside the party line except for the churches. These informal gatherings spawned the 'peace prayers' at the Nicolaikirche every Monday at 5pm. Other churches joined the burgeoning prayer movement and, in addition to the Mondays that by this time were attracting up to two thousand people, they held candle-lit prayer vigils and marches through the streets, particularly in Leipzig on Mondays, and in some areas on Fridays.

The government reacted. From May 8th 1989, access roads to the Nicolaikirche were checked and blocked by police. Later, the autobahn exits to Leipzig were subject to large-scale checks or even closed during the time of the prayers for peace. There were regular arrests or 'temporary detentions'. Yet the people continued to gather and grow, and the movement spread.

In August 1989 Hungary removed its border restrictions and more than 13,000 people left East Germany by crossing the so-called green border via Czechoslovakia into Hungary and then on to Austria and West Germany. The prayer movement continued to grow and was supported by a number of non-Christians.

On October 7th, in a speech prepared for the 40th anniversary of communism in East Germany, their dictator Erich Honecker loudly and proudly proclaimed that the Berlin Wall would stand for another 100 years and repeated the Marxist position that communism would ultimately triumph and rule the world. The party was strong and there was no need for any help, whether secular or especially divine. The Christian faith and the church were an irrelevant leftover from the past and would soon fade away. A popular slogan in the agricultural collectives was *Without God and without sun, we will get the harvest done*. But Honecker's speech was to be his swansong and the generation of communist power was about to come to an abrupt and unexpected end.

By September 1989, the 2,000-seater Nicolaikirche was filled and tens of thousands gathered in the square awaiting the end of the meeting. All participants held lighted candles in their hands and set out towards the city ring road. It is estimated that 300,000 people joined the march past the Stasi headquarters in protest. In the first days of October, leading up to the anniversary, the authorities reacted strongly and for over ten hours uniformed police assaulted unarmed people and took them away in trucks. Hundreds were locked up in stables and the communist press published a strongly-worded article calling for an end to the Western/Zionist-inspired 'counter-revolution' by all means necessary.

On October 9th, orders were issued to shoot the 'counter-revolutionaries'. At least 1,000 communist party members were ordered to attend the Nicholaikirche and some 600 had already filled the church nave by 2pm. Their job was to perform like the Stasi personnel who were on hand regularly and in great numbers at the peace prayers. And so it was that these people heard the Beatitudes read before those who had been able to enter the church departed to join tens of thousands waiting outside.

In the event, no firearms were deployed. On Monday, October 16th, the peace prayers continued and 120,000 people were in the streets of Leipzig demanding democracy and free elections. On October 18th, Erich Honecker resigned. Non-violent protests were held all over Germany including a massive rally in East Berlin on November 4th. On November 7th the entire government of the German Democratic Republic resigned, and on November 9th the crossing points of the Wall in East Berlin opened. Seven months later the entire border regime of the GDR (symbolised by Checkpoint Charlie) came to an end. On October 3rd 1990 Germany was reunified. It was a great privilege to be associated with the movement.

Natasha was an early and long-serving member of Maim Haim, the dance team that performed short dramas and traditional dances in costume in Jewish community centres and churches. The team travelled throughout the Ukraine, UK and Western Europe. I often accompanied them to do the teaching. Here is Natasha's story:

> I attended the Word of Life Bible College in Estonia where I first heard about Israel and the Jewish people. Upon my return to Ukraine, I met my sister Oxana's friend Inga, who was working as a courier with Good News Travels (Exobus in the UK) and was also leading a dance troupe named Maim Chaim from the Hebrew term for 'living water'.

The group generally consisted of three or four girls and two boys who were based in Kiev, my home city. It seemed right almost immediately to be a part of this work. After a time of prayer, it became a reality. We first started by going to Jewish communities all over the Ukraine, many of which were in distant places and very hard to reach due to lack of decent roads, in some cases not even proper roads. We made all of our own costumes and danced traditional Jewish dances from different countries of the world. In addition, we also collected local Jewish traditional dances from place to place as we travelled. In one part of the programme we showed a video about life in Israel to encourage local Jewish people to make aliyah! The response was amazing. Most of them had little or no connection with their Jewish heritage, let alone having ever seen pictures of Israel. Under communism there had been a lot of negative propaganda concerning Israel; the thrust being that people were starving and living in squalor! Seeing the video really stirred a desire to go! As time went by, we added another series of geographically-related videos showing how those from their own areas had settled in the land. These videos were referred to as 'Two Spies' from the two spies who gave a positive report about the land. This helped them to see not just the land, but life there and, on occasion, people they knew.

We also had the opportunity to visit Ukrainian churches. The approach here obviously had to be different. We wanted Christians to know God's heart for his people and the role of believers in it. So we performed our dances and then spoke about the biblical remit for aliyah and God's plan for his representative people.

In the summer of 1997 we had a conference just outside Kiev with the whole team of Good News Travels and invited guests. Dr Fred Wright was invited to teach us at a deep level about the biblical remit for aliyah, the differing types of Jewish identity and practice, the history and causes of anti-Semitism and God's plan for modern Israel. It was a real eye-opener for me in lots of ways because you wouldn't hear teaching like that in any church in

Ukraine. The few days spent there gave me an even greater desire and heart for blessing and helping the people of Israel, along with the rest of the team. We set about devising a drama, 'God, the Church and Israel.' Thus prepared, it gave us an open door into Europe, especially in the UK where we undertook intensive touring, ministering in at least one church a day for over thirty days at a time, accompanied by Fred. We also went to churches in France, Belgium, Holland, Germany, Ireland and Scotland. It was hard going as often we had to sleep on the bus, wash, iron, repair costumes and set up props on site; not to mention the dance practices that were needed. In addition to practice, we had to adapt the programme to the wildly different sizes of stages, platforms or just simply spaces that were given to us.

Maybe the most memorable moment for me was in one of the small churches in France where, after our message about God's unfailing love for the Jewish people and how the church should treat them with love and care, believers asked for permission to wash our feet as a picture of the Church and Israel! It was very moving experience for all of us.

Natasha is married to Dan, and this is his story:

I have known of the importance of the Jewish people and aliyah for as long as I can remember. From the age of seven, I travelled with my parents throughout Eastern Europe and Israel as they undertook prayer journeys and helped the Jewish people in whatever way they could, wherever they were, even before aliyah was possible. We also travelled throughout the UK teaching churches about the Lord's plan for the Jewish people and their destiny. I recall that this message was not always well received.

I vividly remember the meetings on the field where the Jewish people were not only introduced to the idea of the return to Israel, but also what it meant to be Jewish. It was amazing to see their reactions when the Scriptures and language to which they had been denied access were revealed. I fondly recall numerous Shabbat meals throughout Eastern Europe. The most precious were held at the farm in Poland that we visited on more than one occasion to help.

An outstanding memory concerns the few weeks we spent one summer putting on a roof and meeting like-minded people, some of whom were new to the idea. Gustav and Maria, who ran the project, had a son David who was about my age and we quickly became firm friends. While the adults were building the roof, David and I looked after the sheep and cows. We were so impressed by the huge ladder the team constructed we also built our own smaller version to climb into the pens! At night, after the meal, the two of us slept in the hayloft. It was idyllic for someone my age.

Although I was young, I was fascinated by the after-dinner conversations. There were people of different language groups and nationalities all drawn together by the scriptural prophecies of the return of the Jewish people. The conversations were translated from language to language. After some four weeks, I had picked up enough Polish to be able to get by in day to day conversations around the farm. The young were never excluded from the table and it felt like we were one great big family from everywhere meeting together in the family home. Shabbat was always a special time for us and, needless to say, I played the role of token or surrogate son during numerous Pesach meetings in every country we visited.

As we travelled, we often had to sleep in the van as hotels were few and far between and difficult to book. To me though, it was exciting as you never knew what was coming next. Border guards always looked very menacing. I recall they all wore these very large hats with peaks that came down to their noses and had a cigarette stuck in their mouths at an exact angle. They also carried a weapon in their hands that they used as a pointing stick. On occasions they would almost take the vehicle to pieces, on others they only wanted cigarettes, a pen, coffee, cheese or tinned fruit to speed up the process; or anything else that took their fancy in the vehicle. We were always happy to give them a Bible. We trust that they read it before it was probably sold on the black market.

When we first went to Romania, we did not realise that even though our van had long-range tanks, diesel was virtually unobtainable with fuel in general only available in very few locations in the country. Queues would be several miles long. It could take a week or more of being in line before you got it. I recall near Dej that the line was over six kilometres long and families were taking shifts sitting in their vehicles while other family members brought them food and drink. We obtained fuel by flagging down small diesel-driven petrol bowsers that delivered benzene to local garages. I enjoyed watching the bartering for fuel before the dirty-looking substance was syphoned out into a large container we carried with us.

Over time we visited most of the extermination camps in Eastern Europe to pray. What impacted me most was the first visit to Majdanek, situated just outside Lublin, Poland. The whole place had an eerie stillness about it. I vividly recall being really scared walking through the gates, feeling cold and like I had all my hope and happiness taken away from me. Quite accidentally, we walked into the main gas chamber. It was horrific and, though an unremarkable structure, it made me feel physically sick.

Majdanek was captured as a whole entity in July 1944. Unlike what happened in Auschwitz and some of the other camps, the Nazis had no time to evacuate the camp or burn it and destroy the evidence. One of the barracks contained the shoes of 500,000 Jews from the various ghettos and camps, who entered but did not leave. The sight and smell remain with me to this day. Along with cases full of hair, glasses and other items, the shoes continued to impact me throughout the visit and for days afterwards. It still haunts me.

The crematoria were intact at the top of the hill along with a mountain of ash in a pavilion just outside the gas chambers. I remember feeling enraged by the light-hearted attitude of a small group of Middle-Eastern visitors who were the only other ones beside the ashes. I understood that a great evil had been committed against the Jewish people and I joined in the prayers with understanding and a sense of grief. Madjanek was life-changing. I completely understood the priority of advocacy for the Jewish people and the reasons for aliyah that aroused a passion within me that remains to this day.

A curious thing was that, although I had heard my parents talk about it elsewhere, the revisionist view and denial of the local people seemed strange. The camp was in sight of the town and there was also a ghetto, and a transit ghetto there. When we spoke to them, the locals denied any knowledge of the slaughter that took place there despite the daily feature of massive road and rail transportation. My parents told me that Lublin was one of the hardest places to interface with local believers. Chelm, which was one of the major centres of Jewish culture, is not too far from Lublin. We were thrilled to be there but found strong resistance to the message of aliyah as the few remaining Jewish people wanted to 'restore' the town as a centre of Jewish culture and learning.

I was always thrilled to carry a bag or do whatever I could to help in my own way in those early days when we 'sneaked people out' – a passion which continued when aliyah became a possibility. As an adult, I worked on the project for a while and it was in doing so that I met my wonderful wife Natasha.

Dan is of course our son.

Chapter 11

CSA Ministries

Essentially there have been four major carrying ministries; three of them based in the UK: Exobus, Ebenezer and Ezra. Ebenezer's story has been written by their founder and CEO, the late Gustav Scheller of blessed memory.

Ezra International was founded in 1995 as a response to one of the most difficult areas in the aliyah process, namely documentation. Mel Hoezle, founder and president of the organisation, became aware that the main cause of delays, bottlenecks and inability to proceed was due to the sourcing of the required documents to leave the fSU and its satellites. Mel is a former businessman in the USA who ran franchises in the construction and beauty industry. Here is my version of his story:

Following a near-death experience at sea, he became a believer in Yeshua in 1987. The hand of the Lord was so heavy upon him that he could not leave his home for several months. During this time, in prolonged periods of intercession, he began to have dreams and visions. The most overwhelming of these was a vision of Ezekiel's wheel within a wheel hovering over the earth emitting four beams of light, one to each of the four corners of the world. There were also two groups of people, one large and one small. He enquired in prayer as to who these people might be. The Lord told him that the larger group were the Jewish people while the smaller group were the remnant of the Christian church. From this point, Mel developed a deep interest in Israel and its place in the Scriptures and God's plans.

In the USA, Mel was among the first people to set up meetings to raise support for what would eventually become the Ebenezer Emergency Fund. During a Full Gospel Business Men's conference in the Northwest US, the Holy Spirit directed him to sit next to

Steve Lightle at a breakfast meeting. The two men did not previously know one another, but before breakfast was served Mel felt impressed in the Spirit to raise money for whatever project Steve was working on.

Mel introduced himself and quickly learned that Steve felt led to take a trip to Israel, but did not have funds for it. So Mel said the Holy Spirit had told him to raise the funds needed; and that it was a specific amount which should be used to start the new work Steve was about to embark upon. He took an offering, but the total was several hundred dollars short of the figure Mel had been given. At first he believed that he heard incorrectly. However, a day or two later, a post offering made by cheque cleared the bank and the total was now exactly what Mel had been prompted to raise.

The Holy Spirit spoke to him once more and told him that at some point he would meet a man named Clarence with a bridge, which turned out to be Clarence Wagner at Bridges for Peace. He was also told that he would be in contact with someone from the International Christian Embassy in Jerusalem. Both these words were fulfilled during trips to Jerusalem in the 1990s. His meeting at the Christian Embassy (ICEJ) led to his long-standing cooperation with Michael Utterback. During a period of deep intercession, Mel heard from the Spirit that he would someday be personally involved with helping the Jews of the Soviet Union come home to Israel. This was some years before Ezra's beginning. In the meantime, Mel involved himself with a programme to airlift humanitarian aid into Eastern Europe and embarked upon a ministry of encouraging new believers in the countries to which he had access. On one occasion, whilst helping new believers in Albania, the Lord told him that the time was now right for the anticipated work to begin in Russia.

Mel and Michael travelled to Siberia through China. The trip required a huge amount of faith. There was much trepidation when they boarded the aircraft in China as neither of them spoke any of three major Chinese languages. As they waited for take-off to their next stop (the flight schedule required their staying the night before going on to Siberia), the seat next to them remained empty. They were praying for the Lord to help them as they had no-one to meet them and make provision for them during their upcoming layover. Just before take-off, a young woman came to sit in the empty seat. She was wearing a cross! Mel pointed to the cross and said, 'I can see you are the same as me!' She spoke some English and was clearly the Lord's provision for them, helping Mel and Michael as they looked for accommodation upon arriving at their destination.

Once in Siberia, Mel, Michael and a local contact visited several churches. On one occasion, Mel spoke at a church in Irkutsk. While the interpreter shared his message, Mel was somewhat alarmed to see that members of the congregation were starting to cry and getting down on their knees to pray. Mel asked the pastor if he had said something wrong. 'No, no, you don't understand,' the pastor explained. 'Six months ago, during worship, we were given a word of prophecy that three men would come to our church and give us money to help the Jewish people go home. What you are doing today is the fulfilment of that word.' There was great rejoicing and encouragement all round.

Every process should have a beginning, a middle and an end, which is also the case with aliyah. There are several Christian organisations that help in many ways within the land of Israel. The following are those directly linked with, or in relationship with, CSA ministries.

One of Ezra's main partners in ministry, working on the ground as well as raising financial support, is Ministry to Israel led by Michael Utterback, one of the longest-serving workers in CSA. MTI is a biblically-based Christian organisation founded in 1988 and is active in supporting and assisting the return of the Jewish people to Israel through their Final Exodus programme working largely in partnership with Ezra. Realising that helping the Jewish people return to their home to Israel is not the only calling for MTI, the Jerusalem Support Centre was established in 1997 for the purpose of being a witness of Christian love and comfort to the Jewish people in Israel. The staff work daily with Jewish immigrants meeting any number of needs that may arise, wherever possible.

Two special projects are the 'Lone Soldier Programme' that cares for soldiers who have no family, which can be a very lonely place to be. In partnership with the Jewish Agency, the Jerusalem Support Center (JSC) is providing assistance for Israeli soldiers who have no family living with them in Israel. Although they live on a base or in barracks while on active duty, they do not have any family with whom they can stay when they go off duty. So on a monthly salary of just $100 many are forced to rent an apartment and maintain its expenses whilst not on duty.

Other initiatives are the provision of warm clothing for when the lone soldiers are serving on Mt Hermon which is probably the coldest place in the land. Water carrying equipment and any additional clothing and supplies they need whilst serving elsewhere are also provided. In addition, when on leave they are taken out for a meal in a good restaurant, which is a real blessing for them.

Many of the olim from the fSU arrive with very little or nothing. The needs of pregnant women are a particular challenge. A layette package and whatever else is needed following birth is to hand as the expenses involved are more than challenging for the recently arrived.

Here is Michael's story:

The Lord began dealing with me regarding Israel in 1980. I was involved in a Christian ministry, working as Director of Youth and Christian Education in a particular denomination for the State of Washington. Although it was a worthwhile venture, I became restless in my spirit knowing there was more to my life. I began seeking the Lord for hours daily and fasting at times. In April of 1982 I was given a profound life-changing vision and a calling to the Jewish people and the land of Israel. I left the work in Washington State and pastored a church in Miami, Florida, for the next six years, unaware that there were over 250,000 Jews living in that area before accepting the post.

As yet, aliyah was not on my radar, though I had heard of people praying for and protesting on behalf of the Russian Jewish people who were locked in the monolith and were referred to as *Refusniks*.

In 1985 I visited Jerusalem and stayed in an apartment that my church rented. One night, the Lord gave me a dream regarding aliyah from the Former Soviet Union. In the dream I had left Germany and was in the foyer of a large, very cold Russian hotel standing in a circle with others, our hands joined, and we were praying. After the prayer, we walked out of the side doors of the hotel and went up the driveway. I was following the others when the Lord instructed me to turn right. I then went up a green grassy hill and looked down on a large group of buses standing side by side. On the sides of the buses the names of Eastern bloc countries were written in 50% grey. In the middle was a bus with the word POLAND written in big, black, block letters. I got on the bus and sat waiting for people to come. After a while I became agitated. I got off the bus and went through the front doors of the hotel. To the left was a large desk and a woman sitting in a chair looking away. I asked her, 'Where are the Jews that are supposed to be on these buses?' She turned in slow motion and, with an amplified voice, said very loudly, 'It is not time yet!' It was enough to wake me up!

Saturated in the presence of the Lord, I began writing every detail of the vision in a spiral notebook. At the time, I had no real understanding of how any of this was to be accomplished. There was an Iron Curtain around all these countries and I couldn't then imagine how it could possibly come down.

From then on, I challenged people to pray for the return of the Jews from the fSU. I was also becoming increasingly involved with the International Christian Embassy Jerusalem, especially with the leadership. Asked to be an international representative, I left the

Miami church in 1988 to start a work called Ministry to Israel for the denomination I served.

In 1990 the Lord prompted me to share the vision of aliyah from the fSU that I had received in 1985 with the leadership of the ICEJ. Of course the Iron Curtain was still intact, so it wasn't all that well received. But in 1991, just after it collapsed, I was in the US on a speaking tour when I received a call from the director of the ICEJ, Johann Luckoff, telling me there was a gentleman in his office, Phil Hunter, who was owner of a bus company in England called Good News Travels. He proceeded to tell me that Phil was offering to use his buses to transport Jews from the fSU to airports in other countries to be flown to Israel. I rushed to Israel to meet Phil who in the meantime approached the Jewish Agency with his offer. He was told the JA were working in Vienna, but that there was a need in Warsaw and that it would be good to work from there into the Ukraine. To me this was particularly significant, bearing in mind the vision where the first bus I saw was 'POLAND'. The ICEJ rented premises outside of Warsaw as a base of operations for Good News Travels and this is where I initially met Pat Frame who was based there.

I was appointed as Director of Aliyah by the leadership of the ICEJ and began working closer with Phil and his team of bus drivers and couriers, travelling in and out on the buses and raising funds in many countries. For many years I continued in this work with the ICEJ as well as directing the work of Ministry to Israel where aliyah was one of the main topics of endeavor.

In my opinion, Steve Lightle certainly heard from the Lord, but I think, as with all visions, there is a timing issue. I was personally involved in, and saw first-hand, the flow of Jews from Russia to Finland and the amazing network of churches and Christian families set up by the ICEJ. Finnish branch director Dr Ulla Jarvellheto and her team are worthy of particular mention. Tens of thousands of Jews were brought through that nation, being housed for three to four days with Christian families throughout Finland before being brought to the airport at Helsinki for the final portion of their journey to Israel.

Of course, all of us have various opinions about the work of aliyah. When I first got involved, I thought most Jews would already be home by now. Watching the slowing numbers through the years has affected the momentum for fundraising. Also, there were a number of organisations keen to work on aliyah in those early days that have now closed down while others never really got off of the ground despite flurries of fundraising.

From my perspective, I think that this is a time of preparation for another wave of incoming Jews who will experience, perhaps in a more excruciating way, being forced to come. It's like Gideon's small army; it is a time for spreading our network throughout countries from where potential olim will be coming. Secondly, we must also broaden our base of financial support and, thirdly, we must stand as a beacon of warning to those Jews sitting on the fence of indecision.

It is my sense that there is a great wave of aliyah coming in the next few years. With the rise of anti-Semitism in France, Belgium, Germany, Hungary, Great Britain and other countries as well, it is a certainty that more and more Jews will look to the Jewish State of Israel as a haven. I think the most shocking event that will stir Jewish communities is the possible economic collapse of certain nations or perhaps the severe decline of the dollar and the euro across the globe, causing many to lose their fortunes.

I also strongly believe the seductive wealth of the West is like the fleshpots of Egypt for which the Israeli slaves longed once they were on their way home in the first Exodus. In the United States in particular, materialism and wealth are the chains keeping Jews from making aliyah. Once those chains are broken, our Jewish brethren will look towards the shores of the Promised Land.

A notable event happened the first time I went to Uzbekistan to explore ways to help the Jewish community make aliyah from that nation. I went to the Jewish Agency director, David Greenberg, and spent the morning with him discussing how we could help. He told me they needed transportation to bring Jews from other cities to Tashkent for processing and for flights to Israel. Very enthusiastically I said, "Don't worry, we'll get you a bus!"

After leaving his office, the reality of where we were started to sink in and I couldn't believe I made such a foolish promise. As I travelled back to Finland where I was to meet Dr Jarvellheto, I worried the entire time about just how I would get a bus to Uzbekistan, two thousand miles away. As we sat at lunch, very sheepishly I told Ulla the story. She began to laugh. I asked why she was laughing and she proceeded to tell me that a Finnish man who owned buses had given them a bus but it wasn't registered in Finland so they weren't sure what use it would be there. She accepted the bus, wondering what to do with it. The registration in Russia was exactly what we needed to get the bus registered in Uzbekistan.

Dr Jarvellheto arranged a team of two drivers to take a bus filled with spare parts for the bus (most important there as you could not get spares there or anywhere nearby) from the Finnish border all the way to Tashkent. We then found a driver and agreed to pay his salary, relieving the Jewish Agency of this burden. For many years that bus, with no windows, was used to transport thousands of Jews. In due time it was traded for a much better one and to this day we are still maintaining a bus and paying the salary of the driver. Today, however, not only is it used to transport olim to Tashkent for flights, but it is also used to bring young Jewish people to study at a computer training centre that we have provided. There they learn about life in Israel, job opportunities, social events, history and, more importantly, they study Hebrew.

The first time I met Ruth, James, Steve and Sib was on a trip to Kiev. I was to stay with them at the infamous Roach Motel in downtown Kiev, so named as the cockroaches outnumbered the guests. It was actually a quaint, dirty-to-the-core, apartment rented for the Fishermen, with many creatures running around as though they owned the place (I think actually they did). We went out one day with Sib as our tour guide. He had an old book of facts which, before each stop, he would stand and read with his back to us. He then quickly placed the book in his pouch, straightened up and with a theatrical turn, hands clasped one on top of the other, he said, 'Now then!' Pointing out various places with flowing gestures, he began sharing the historical facts of whatever place we happened to be. His performance was endearing and drew a few warm-hearted comments from our little group that made us all chuckle.

At the Roach Motel there was a boys' and a girls' side for sleeping. Since there was no more room on the boys' side, and me being older than everyone else, I was placed on the girls' side which happened to be Ruth's area. From then on, I was known as Ruth's roomie. You can imagine the eyebrows being raised when I was introduced to someone new who didn't know the circumstances. To this day, every time we see each other, that invariably comes up.

I have never been personally attacked for my stance on behalf of Israel. Of course, there have been verbal exchanges with anti-Semitic views. Once in Red Square I was watching a neo-Nazi march of a few hundred young men dressed in uniform with swastikas and various emblems. I began taking pictures and was seen by the leader who promptly came over and began yelling. In English, he asked who I was. I told him I was writing a story for our newsletter, which I was, and needed pictures. He seemed proud that the group was getting attention from a 'reporter' from the United States and began expounding their creed and telling me who they were. Basically, it came down to one thing. He said, 'We hate Jews and we hate blacks!' I then asked, 'Are you like Hitler?' He said, 'We are better Nazis than Hitler.' After a few more questions, at a convenient moment, I retreated to a safer place.

I also recollect two occasions when there was picketing by pro-Palestinian factions in front of the buildings where I was invited to speak at Cambridge, England, and the Parliament building in

Northern Ireland called Stormont. There were no incidents and police were on hand to monitor the situations. We were once also picketed by Jews for Jews outside a building in Baltimore, Maryland.

Interestingly, in Israel, I have mentioned to many people what we do and how we help the poorest of the poor to make aliyah and settle in the land. In earlier days it was usually accepted, with a "Thank you for what you do". But in recent times, even this past week, I've had people ask why we are doing this. One middle-aged taxi driver told me, with a raised voice, that it is hurting the economy of Israel. He said when older people come they drain the nation's funds and that competition for work was horrible, pointing out there were over five thousand taxi drivers in Jerusalem alone. I then asked if he had come from another country, to which he replied no but that his parents had come from Europe.

Paul said, 'Now if their fall is riches for the world, and their failure riches for the Gentiles, how much more their fullness?' (Romans 11:12). The Amplified Bible puts it this way: 'Now if their stumbling (their lapse, their transgression) has so enriched the world [at large], and if [Israel's] failure means such riches for the Gentiles, think what an enrichment and greater advantage will follow their full reinstatement!' These promises cannot be fulfilled as long as the Jews are scattered throughout the world. Therefore, the work we do is probably one of the more vital dimensions of Christian ministry.

Craig came to Ezra from Bridges for Peace and looked after the work in Latin America. Here is Craig's story followed by an account of this exciting work:

You wouldn't usually associate the Greyhound bus company with aliyah, but it was during a cross-country trip on one of their coaches that I was introduced to the prophecies and scriptures promising the Jewish people's end-time return to Eretz Israel.

I had just finished four years of work as an English teacher in western Ukraine. Before starting work at a new job in northern California, I returned home to the Midwest to visit my family. Greyhound was the least expensive option for a poor teacher, and my trek took me across the Sierra Nevada mountains and toward the Rockies. The scenery was spectacular, but during the trip I found my attention drawn to a part of the Bible I had not studied carefully before. It was a wonderful read, starting in Isaiah 40. Reading through these chapters, I was comforted and encouraged by the promises I found there. I found a few 'life verses' there as well. It didn't occur to me that most of those verses were originally directed to the people of Israel!

A few years later, while studying at Bible College, I noted that several of the courses focused on Israel's story as related in the Tanakh, the Old Testament. One of my professors travelled there every year and, as I finished my last semester with her, she urged me to plan a trip to Israel as soon as I could go. 'I'll go there after the Lord returns,' I told her. 'There are other places I'd rather go first!'

At the time, I was fairly certain that Russia would be one of those places. The following academic year saw me undertaking study in grammar and linguistics in order to prepare me for what I prayed and hoped would be an opportunity to join Bible translation initiatives in the Caucasus Mountains.

My path to serving on such a project took an unexpected turn, though, when I was diagnosed with a form of cancer in the brain. I had an operation and entered treatment. I realised my plans for any future ministry would have to change. During some difficult months of prayer and reflection, I found a place of peace with this change. Following one weekend spent in intense prayer, I asked God to make clear his plan for me. The answer came while I was watching a ministry leader interviewed on Christian TV. He described their teams' work assisting Jewish people from the former Soviet Union as they prepared to move to Israel.

I was fascinated as he described the process of finding and translating documents, searching for long-lost records in the archives, and helping transport Jewish families to the airport. While I lived in Ukraine in the late 1990s, I had done something very similar for Christian friends preparing to leave for the US. This might be a way in which I could serve!

After contacting the ministry, Bridges for Peace, I began to study Israel more intensely. In 2008 I started service in Jerusalem with Bridges for Peace. My background in the Ukraine led to an assignment with the ministry's programmes for olim. I served both in Jerusalem and in the country's northern part before finishing my time in Israel in 2010.

As I left Bridges for Peace that summer, CEO Becky Brimmer recommended I contact Mel Hoezle at Ezra International. I did, and within a year I was working with aliyah programmes, coming into contact with olim not only from Ukraine and Russia, but also South America and Central Asia.

My responsibilities included coordinating Ezra's work in Latin America. With hundreds of thousands of Jewish people in Argentina, Brazil, Uruguay, Mexico and other countries of the region, we have our work cut out for us. But God, His love, and His promises are still the same and He is bringing the Jewish people home from the farthest corners of the earth.

Latin American tensions

Ezra International's work in Latin America dates back to the end of 2001 when a severe economic crisis in Argentina, and a dramatic increase in aliyah, prompted the Jewish Agency to call for all hands on deck. Several aliyah ministries responded but it proved to be a nut that was hard to crack. Ezra provided assistance not only to new olim but also to yordim – Jewish people who had made aliyah but for various reasons had returned to their home country, usually Argentina.

Since 2002, Ezra International has helped both olim and yordim make their way back to the Promised Land. Most of the Jewish families assisted thus far are from Argentina. Others have come from neighbouring countries including Chile, Uruguay, Panama and Brazil. At the time of writing Venezuela, once considered a safe place for Jewish people but now in political meltdown, is of great concern.

Although Buenos Aires was the target of terrible anti-Israel violence in the mid-1990s, including a terror bombing of the city's Jewish cultural centre, few of the olim leaving the country in recent years have cited violence or discrimination as their motive for making aliyah – though Argentina again faces political and economic instability. Once more, many Jewish families see aliyah not only as an option but also as a necessity – a chance to secure a stable future for themselves and their children.

Ezra International has expanded its presence not only in Argentina but also in Brazil and other Latin American countries. Argentina remains a major focus for aliyah as its Jewish population of more than 180,000 is South America's largest concentration of Jewish people.

Brazil too has sizeable Jewish communities in Sao Paulo and Rio de Janeiro while neighbouring Uruguay is home to over 20,000 Jews. In each of these nations, one important focus of aliyah ministry is 'fishing'. Many secular Jewish people who do not identify closely with Israel or with their local Jewish communities may not realise that aliyah is both their opportunity and their right. As in other countries, Jewish families living outside of the capital cities find themselves cut off from activities sponsored by the Israeli consulate, the Jewish Agency or by other aliyah-promoting organisations.

Information about the Law of Return, the documents needed to prove one's Jewishness, and the benefits associated with making aliyah, can be the deciding factor for many potential olim. Fishing teams will have their work cut out in the near future as the God of Israel brings the Jewish people of Latin America home.

Ezra leaders very often have meetings with senior leaders of the Jewish Agency asking the question, 'Is there anything else we can do?' In April 2012 Mel Hoezle, along with Michael Utterback, met with one of their senior people, Yehudah, in the JA offices in Jerusalem along with other Ezra team members and JA staff. They talked over various issues and then Mel asked the above question and received a request to help a most unusual and interesting group of Jewish people.

In the remote reaches of Peru, where the largest city in the Peruvian rainforest is located, surrounded by three rivers – the Nanay, the Itaya and the Amazon – dwell one of the most geographically remote Jewish communities in the world. Every Jewish community is unique, but the history of Iquitos' Jewish descendants is so exceptional that it almost sounds fictional, says Dr Ariel Segal, a Venezuelan-born Israeli scholar now teaching at a university in the Peruvian capital of Lima. The city can only be reached either by river or air but not by road as they do not exist! The Jewish presence in the Amazon was established by Moroccan Jews who arrived in 1810 from Fez, Tangier, Tetuan, Casablanca, Salé, Rabat and Marrakesh. In 1824 the first synagogue, Essel Avraham, was organised in Belém. The peak of the boom in the rubber industry between 1880 and 1910 coincided with the height of Jewish immigration from Europe. Communities sprang up along the Amazon River, in particular the regions of Santarém and Manaus.

Groups led by German Jewish merchants eventually ventured as far as Iquitos in search of rubber. Many families lived in isolated *ribeirinhos* settlements. An early rabbi became something of a legend. Rabino Shalom Imanuel-Muyal was considered a holy man who was admired, even by non-Jews, as a healer and became a folklore saint. To this day he is referred to as Santo Moisézinho (Saint Little Moses).

As time passed the community became isolated due to a caste-type system from colonialism which saw Amazonians, who spoke Ladino, Hebrew and Haketia (an almost extinct Jewish-Moroccan language) considered inferior, resulting in a virtual lack of interaction for many years. In 1905 the Jewish immigrants, who initially had no intention of staying long, built a cemetery to accommodate the inevitable loss of life in a frontier area whilst refraining from building such permanent structures as a synagogue or a school. In the event, by 1909, they had founded and formally registered the Israelite Society of Beneficence of Iquitos in order to provide assistance to fellow Jews. In reality they only met for the celebration of the Jewish high holidays and scarcely developed a local Jewish life or society.

Most of the Jewish people, in common with most of the other immigrants, married or had children with local Amazonian women. During the 1910s, with the decline of rubber prices, a good number of the Jews left the city and drifted to the USA. Those who stayed, together with the first generation of their descendants, met occasionally for Sabbath services in private homes. Although they continued to intermarry with local Christian natives, the descendants of Jews preserved a strong sense of Jewishness, kept up some Jewish traditions and made several attempts to sustain a fragile community, which made its first contacts with Lima's Jews during the 1950s after a gap of several decades.

Subsequently they re-engaged more actively with their Jewish background and began to aspire to move to Israel, but the immediate question of Jewish heritage, blood and rights of return surfaced and produced high tension. Scant interest was paid by the wider Jewish world for a good number of years. But around twelve years ago, 250 of the community members underwent a Conservative conversion process and were able to make aliyah.

At the time of writing there are a total of 284 Peruvians from Iquitos who were formally converted to Judaism by a Conservative rabbinical court in August 2011 after engaging in Jewish studies for five years. It is this group with whom Ezra engaged. The first 100 arrived in Israel in 2013 and a further 150 in 2014. Under current immigration procedures, individuals who are not born Jewish under rabbinical law are expected to spend nine months as an active member of their local Jewish communities. After they have completed the conversion process, regardless of what type of conversion they have undergone, they can move to Israel. During this time, their applications are reviewed by the Interior Ministry, which does not have its own emissaries abroad, and typically relies on recommendations from the Jewish Agency as to the validity of conversions performed abroad. Ezra plays a significant role in this matter as they are the key ministry in finding and providing documents to authenticate their status.

The Jewish Agency last year notified the Interior Ministry that it had determined that the conversions performed for the group of 284 Peruvians had been satisfactorily fulfilled. All of the necessary criteria to make them eligible for immigrating to Israel under the Law of Return was in place. Ministry officials had initially insisted, despite a JA legal ruling to the contrary, that bringing such a large group of 'so-called' converts to Israel required a special cabinet meeting. Both JA officials and Conservative movement leaders in Israel were incensed by the Interior Ministry's refusal to grant the Peruvians permission to immigrate. After withholding approval for several months, they eventually accepted the legal ruling that no cabinet decision was required in order to bring the group over.

Another difficulty, Yehudah explained, was that primary movement to an international airport by the Jewish people coming by air from Iquitos could only be accompanied by one 30kg suitcase. They would be coming to empty homes when they arrived in Israel! He asked if Ezra could help them upon arrival in Israel as they would need almost everything. Mel and Michael immediately committed to help with $20,000 dedicated to buying electrical and other household goods for these families when they arrived in Israel. At least forty of the families were helped in this way.

As Ministry to Israel is based in Jerusalem, their team did the 'on the ground work' with these new immigrants. Michael recalls: One day we took over an appliance store with 20 Peruvian olim, going from item to item with each family. It was exciting for the newcomers but was also touching for the store owner and sales people who helped us. The owner asked me to come to her office, which I did. She told me how overwhelming it was for Christians to be doing something like this and wanted to thank me personally. I then told her that all the finances were coming from Christians in various countries. In addition, it's hard to explain the childlike sweetness of the Peruvian Jews. They were so appreciative for all we did and they were rather overwhelmed at the generosity.

Ezra International's other main partner in ministry is Bridges for Peace. Dr Douglas Young (1910-1979), seminary dean and professor of Old Testament at Dropsie College, Philadelphia, Pennsylvania, felt that it was necessary for pastors and individual Christians to get better acquainted with Israel, to come to the land, to study, and to get involved with the land and its people. To this end he founded Bridges for Peace which, in 1978, was introduced in the US and later in Canada.

Upon Dr Young's untimely death in 1979, Clarence Wagner Jr assumed directorship of the work, which soon began a period of rapid growth and expansion into many other countries. Today it is headed up by Becky Brimmer. Their original small publication, *Dispatch from Jerusalem*, was greatly enlarged and changed from a quarterly to a bi-monthly publication. In 1985, Bridges began Operation Ezra (Ezra means help in Hebrew), a social assistance program allowing Christians everywhere to become personally involved in helping Israelis, particularly new immigrants.

In the ten-year period beginning from 1990, Bridges assisted at least 20,000 new immigrant families upon their arrival in Israel. These families were supplied, from the 'Bridges Food Bank', with food baskets, blankets, kitchen utensils and many other items. As they entered the twenty-first century, the organisation was assisting around 2,400 families each month while also distributing 31 metric tons (31,000 kilos) of food. Through their programmes, hundreds of families have now been 'adopted' for regular support by Christian families abroad. Hundreds of homes of Holocaust survivors, new immigrants and the poor have been repaired by the Bridges home repair team.

On two occasions, they have received special recognition by the city of Jerusalem for outstanding work in the area of social assistance. Through Project Rescue, BFP offer financial support for Ezra International to facilitate aliyah.

The International Christian Embassy Jerusalem has been a key player from the start of CSA. In July 1980, Israel declared Jerusalem as its eternal indivisible capital. Under the threat of an Arab oil embargo, all thirteen national embassies representing Western nations in Jerusalem relocated to Tel Aviv. Two months later, in solidarity with Israel, Christians from 23 nations founded the International Christian Embassy Jerusalem. Today the embassy has representation in more than 100 nations and a staff of 60 multi-national volunteers based at its Jerusalem headquarters. In addition to advocacy for Israel, they run a number of social projects including a home for holocaust survivors.

ICEJ have been very active in recent years helping the remaining Jews of Ethiopia and the Jewish people of India to return. Their annual celebration of the Feast of Tabernacles and the March of the Nations through Jerusalem is a highlight of the year for those who love Israel and the Jewish people.

Historically they have provided money to the JA for flights and transportation, via the ministry of Exobus in the early years and, latterly, wherever there has been an emergency for aliyah.

Jerusalem Vistas is the ministry of Jay and Meridel Rawlings who forsook their careers in hospital administration and nursing to pursue their vision for aliyah, moving their family to Israel in 1969. Their burning desire was to become and recruit 'fishers' based upon their understanding of Jeremiah 16:16. In this cause, they visited Jewish communities in some 120 countries. Their remarkable story was later related in their book entitled *Fishers and Hunters*.

Jay turned down a job offer as administrator of the second largest hospital in Israel in order to bring the story of Israel to Christians on film. His production, *Apples of Gold,* was shown worldwide and was even placed in Israeli Foreign Ministry offices around the globe. The film was followed in 1986 by *Gates of Brass*, a documentary making known the plight of Jews behind the Iron Curtain. Within three years of the film's release, the Rawlings were able to rejoice as thousands of Soviet Jews began making their way home to Israel.

The electronic tool for their work was established in Jerusalem in 1982 and is now called Jerusalem Vistas and Israel Vision. The latter is their regular television programme that reaches 130 million viewers in 60 countries. The Rawlings family continue to be great friends of Israel and two of their sons have served in the Israeli Defense Forces.

Christian Friends of Israel is an evangelical para-church ministry also with its headquarters in Jerusalem with affiliate offices throughout the world. CFI was established in 1985 by co-founders Ray and Sharon Sanders. The ministry has a very effective programme of educating the church in the UK and elsewhere in addition to aid-related programmes in the land.

During the Gulf War of 1991, when great numbers of new immigrants were arriving in the land, CFI went into action to provide help in the resettling process for these immigrants. Clothing, both new and used, was secured from abroad and transported to Israel by loving Christian hands. The clothing was then sorted and distributed at the CFI centre. To date, they have supplied over 200 tons of clothing to more than 130,000 new immigrants.

A very important and attractive part of the CFI Distribution Centre's work is that of helping new immigrants to enjoy a beautiful wedding as many arrive without funding for their special day. The ministry helps by lending wedding gowns free of charge to new immigrant brides, along with suitable outfits for bridesmaids, maids of honour and groomsmen – all donated by Christians from the nations.

CFI also sponsors other outreach projects to Israel. Holiday gift parcels are made up for IDF soldiers defending the nation. A Holocaust Fund helps hundreds of needy survivors with financial aid and Christian love, and an annual Holocaust Remembrance Day is sponsored in order to share the healing balm of God's love with many who suffered in and throughout the Holocaust.

Christians for Israel (C4I) was established in 1979 in Holland and Jerusalem under the leadership of Karel van Oordt and the late Pee Koelewijn. The initial vision was to bring a biblical understanding to the church and the nations of God's purposes concerning Israel, and to provide support and comfort to Israel and the Jewish people both in prayer and action.

In the mid-1990s, by means of newspapers available in the main European languages, the message was spread within central Europe. C4I has been a major funding agency for the carrying ministries and, in addition, has supported a number of projects within the land.

For several years, they have also had a small team based in west Ukraine helping with aliyah, primarily driving Jewish people to airports where they catch flights to Israel. They also seek opportunities to teach about Israel and aliyah in the churches.

Chapter 12
Hindrances and Objections to CSA

Hindrances to aliyah can be arbitrarily divided into two sections – religious and secular – with the sub-divisions of Jewish and Christian. In the first case, political and philosophical, in the latter largely anti-Semitic.

Jewish Objections

Jewish religious objections to aliyah are bound within the Jewish objections to the messiahship of Yeshua. In Judaism, the emphasis is not upon the person of the Moshiach, but upon the messianic task, kingdom and rule. Jewish people reject the messiahship of Yeshua on three basic grounds:

1 He did not gather the galut (exile)
2 He did not rebuild the Temple
3 He did not institute the reign of peace on earth

As the task of the ingathering is that of the Messiah, [in some instances] both the state of Israel and aliyah are theological aberrations. Worse still, Zionism in its non-pejorative form, in all its various stripes, is rebellion against G-d. This was the initial view of some of the leading rebbes during World War II who saw the Holocaust as God's punishment for usurping the Messiah's task (see *Father Forgive Us* by Fred Wright for a full discussion).

A second strand of objection is that Christian-sponsored aliyah is a passive form of crusade.

Christian objections

The main Christian objections are found in so-called Replacement Theology, sometimes known as supercessionism, which arises from three main sources.

Firstly, the anti-Semitic writings of the Church Fathers, the Scholastic movement and the Reformation, in particular Martin Luther (see *The Dark Legacy of Martin Luther* by Fred Wright).

Secondly, Dispensationalism, a scheme of eschatology followed by nearly all Pentecostals, independent Charismatics, Brethren and Southern Baptists posits that the state of Israel and the return and salvation of the Jewish people takes place after the Lord's return. Dispensationalism also teaches the non-biblical 19th century-initiated doctrine of the rapture and two second comings (see *Eschatology, Origins and Consequences*, FW 2019).

The third strand comes from a disregard both of scripture and history that commences with the rejection of the Jewish people following the death of Jesus. One outcome of this is of the vulgar, classical religious anti-Semitic stripe while the other is founded in the liberal view of the scriptures. The historical process, particularly the founding of the state, is subject to revisionism (see *Words from the Scroll of Fire*, FW for a full discussion).

Secular Objections

Most political and attendant sentimental objections to aliyah are in reality objections to the state of Israel, its existence and its relationship with the so-called Palestinians, who are mainly the descendants of illegal Arab immigrants (see *Father Forgive Us*). The main fallacy is the accusation that the Jews stole the Arab native homelands. The myth of seizure and the monsterisation of Israel are usually framed in terms of international law arising from UN resolutions. The subject is vast, but in brief:

In a similar way that the Magna Carta and Habaeus Corpus are the founding documents of British statehood, the Balfour Declaration and the San Remo Conference are the founding documents of the sovereign State of Israel. At the San Remo Conference of April 24, 1920, the principal allied powers agreed to assign the Mandate for the territory of Palestine to Great Britain. By doing so, the League of Nations recognised the historical connection of the Jewish people with Palestine and established 'grounds for reconstituting their national home in that country'. Article 6 of the Mandate 'encouraged close settlement by Jews on the land, including the lands of Judea, Samaria and Gaza (Yesha)'.

Further to this provision, some 76% of the territory of Mandated Palestine, known today as Jordan, was not permanently exempt from settlement by the Jewish people; Article 25 only allowed to 'postpone or withhold application of [this] provision'.

Resolution 181, in November 1947, recommended the partition of 1946. In Article 80 of its charter, it specifically allowed the continuation of existing mandates (including the British Mandate). Article 80 stated that 'nothing ... shall be construed in or of itself to alter in any manner the rights whatsoever of any peoples or the terms of existing international instruments to which members of the United Nations may respectively be parties'.

In common with all UN resolutions pertaining to the Jewish-Arab conflict, it was not enforceable. It was simply a recommendation. Needless to say, the Arab countries rejected it. If the resolution had been implemented, it might have been possible to argue that it replaced the San Remo Conference resolution, which had legitimised the rights of the Jews to settle in any place in Palestine. However, it was not only rejected by the Arabs but, in violation of the UN Charter, they launched military aggression against the newly-reborn Jewish state, thus invalidating the resolution. A fact generally overlooked!

There are different types of resolutions passed by the United Nations. There are in fact two types in the Security Council that are important in this matter. The first are resolutions passed on the basis of Chapter 6 of the UN Charter that relates to the settlement of disputes through peaceful means. Such resolutions are considered recommendations. They are not binding and do not require immediate implementation. The second type are based on Chapter 7 of the UN Charter which gives the UN Security Council resolutions an implementative authority and commits the international community to use force if necessary to implement such. None of the UN Security Council resolutions pertaining to the Arab-Israeli conflict, including Resolution 425, were passed on the basis of Chapter 7. They were passed on the basis of Chapter 6, which is also the basis of resolutions 242 and 338. The erroneously termed 'occupied territories' have become a symbol in the cycle of Palestinian violence.

Reflections upon UN Resolution 242

As the outbreak of war with Iraq loomed, the issue of Palestinian 'freedom' (whatever that is supposed to mean) became inevitably attached to the issue. The matter of Palestinian statehood and Israeli occupation is always framed in terms of UN Security Council resolution 242 which has become the motivation for BDS (the Boycott, Divestment and Sanctions movement) and all opposed to Israel.

Resolution 242 was adopted on November 22, 1967, following the Six Day War, to establish provisions and principles which, it was hoped, would lead to a solution of the conflict. After lengthy discussions, the final draft was presented by the British Ambassador, Lord Caradon. The resolution has become almost iconic in its own right and is possibly the most misinterpreted UN resolution of all time. It calls for 'peace for land' – not 'land for peace'. The formularisation grants every state in the Middle East '...the right to live in peace within secure and recognised boundaries'. The point here is that peace must be established before territorial withdrawal to 'recognised boundaries'. Resolution 242 is not the bogeyman of international law, or the blueprint for a Palestinian state. Self-determination for the Palestinians appears nowhere in the resolution. Neither does the notion of an International Conference to determine the matter(s).

A second important element of Resolution 242 is that it applies to legally constructed national states, not terrorist groups, insurgents or would-be self-appointed governments-in-exile. The phrase 'territories occupied' is not preceded by the definite article, neither is the expression 'on all fronts' involved. It is therefore erroneous to apply Resolution 242 in the way that it is usually presented concerning territories administered by Israel since June 1967. It is also clear that the so-called 'occupied territories' do technically fall into the definition of that term as embedded in 242. In reality, Israel does not hold any 'occupied' territories. The Security Council, in its own words, was expressing its continuing concern with the grave situation in the Middle East, emphasising the inadmissibility of the acquisition of territory by war and the need to work for a just and lasting peace in which every state in the area can live in security.

A particularly subtle form of anti-Semitism has insinuated its way into recent thought, and to some extent has found its success in Post-Modernist-Post-Zionist thinking (henceforth PMPZ), much of which is due to a phenomenon which, for convenience, we will term auto-anti-Semitism or racial self-loathing. In the same way that an individual can experience self-revulsion, particularly because of constant rejection, the same dynamic can appear within a social, national or ethnic group. The Jewish people, as the subject of innumerable persecutions, have in some cases reached a point of spiritual and ethnic exhaustion. In Israel this is particularly true due to the tensions of constant militant pressure from the surrounding nations along with political pressure from the West, particularly under the presidency of Barak Obama.

An internal problem focusing around the question of the nature of the state and its people flourishes within Jewish PMPZ adherents. Further tensions surround the role of the diaspora and international relations. The tensions may be expressed thus:

The state and its relationship to Judaism
The nature of the state
The relationship of the state to the diaspora
The state's relationship to the surrounding nations
International relations

Put simply, the argument revolves around the question, 'Should Israel, and especially Jerusalem, be regarded as the worldwide centre of the Jewish faith?' PMPZ would contend that the Jews who live in America are Americans, those who live in Germany are Germans and those in France, French, all of whom practice or have historical associations with the Jewish faith. The Jews in Israel, likewise, are Israelis who either practice, or are associated with, the Jewish faith, or have no faith. The state was born in sin and practices an ethnocentric policy. Israel, if it is to exist (so they argue), should become a plurality and return as much land as is needed to promote peace and harmony.

There is a vast amount of PMPZ literature. It is widely read in the UK, even by Messianics opposed to aliyah who quote these works extensively. One author, Ilan Pappe, lectured at Oxford University.

They argue that Israel forcibly expelled the Palestinians from their homes. Benny Morris first introduced this notion when attempting to write a history of the Palmach but has happily since changed his position though, sadly, he is still often quoted. They further state that Jewish connection to the land has been fabricated, possibly the most outrageous contention as a simple read through the Bible illustrates.

The Holocaust, they say, is an industry with the cynical motive of political gain (Tom Segev), effectively borrowing lines from Holocaust deniers. Zionism was, and remains, a colonial movement in the sense of Western European colonisation.

Chapter 13

The Evangelism of Silence and Grace

A recurring question posed to CSA ministries concerns the wrongly positioned: 'Do you give the Jews [note; never Jewish people] the gospel?' In essence, the question immediately exhibits a complete misapprehension of the biblical and historical understanding of the destiny both of the Jewish people and Christians. A redundant, traditional understanding of Yeshua's teaching of the kingdom, the role of Israel and Jewish people in the drama of salvation, and a flawed hermeneutic that views the whole of the scriptures through a distorted New Testament lens is also an underlying factor for this misunderstanding.

It should, however, be pointed out that there is no formal theology of aliyah. A modest attempt towards this is made in my *Aliyah, Holy to the Lord*. But I am generally suspicious of the motivation of those who ask these sorts of questions. Whereas they can be asked from a position of genuine curiosity, they usually betray some other agenda. Let's firstly consider the people to whom these sorts of things are an issue.

Messianic believers

Those who do not want to make aliyah often wish to use the matter to illustrate that there is something non-Christian at work as it denies the core of their idea of what the gospel means. Those who have made aliyah but failed to settle and returned to their country of origin use it as a tool to defend themselves.

Others, when they became believers in Yeshua, posit that aliyah can only be authentic when the Jewish people get saved outside of the land and then return as believers when the Lord comes back. But this is a really bad misreading of Isaiah 51.

Sure, not to share the gospel is the worst form of anti-Semitism as it consigns the unsaved to hell. But, some say, aliyah ministries put Jewish people in the vulnerable position of potentially falling prey to Jewish orthodoxy.

The Church

Those who hold to replacement theology – self-explanatory.

Basic Christian anti-Semites who think the aim of evangelism is to bring an end to Jewishness.

Those who think that Israel is just another country and the Jewish people simply another people group.

Those who assume the ministries hold to 'Dual Covenant' theology (one for Jews and another for Gentiles).

Dispensationalists: that the Jewish people can't return until Messiah comes back, when they will return in a state of salvation.

There is a lot of misunderstanding around terminology: gospel and evangelism, for example, which are both drawn from the same root. The primary usage of these terms refers to an expression drawn from Middle-English 'god spell' which is a calque (word-for-word translation) of the Greek word *euangelion*. Although referred to as the Gospel of God (or the Gospel of Christ), these expressions are in reality exchange terms for the Gospel of the Kingdom [of God] with special emphasis on Matthew 24:14, which was in fact the *euangelion* preached by Yeshua.

The Kingdom of God is the core of the gospel which centres around both the task of the Messiah and the unfolding of the kingdom. The messianic expectation was that the Messiah would return the exiles, rebuild the Temple and usher in the reign of God. As we await the return of the Messiah, these tasks now fall to the Church as mentioned previously. Aliyah is, therefore, an essential part of the *euangelion*. Yeshua and Shaul both taught that the body is now the temple, so part of the *euangelion* is to build the Temple of the *Ruach h'Kodesh* in the life of the believer and usher in the kingdom by exhibiting its reality in the life of the believer. We are persuaded that this is our part in the *euangelion* and provides a solid foundation for the future in the lives of the olim.

The *euangelion*, therefore, is much more than distributing Bibles or arguing the truth of the scriptures. It is living it out in the sensible world. We are called to make Israel jealous (Romans 11:11). Is there any better way of demonstrating the *euangelion* than by aliyah, which illustrates biblical, kingdom values and a living reality? In the same way that some are called to exhibit the kingdom by worship, acts of mercy or in many diverse ways, CSA ministries believe that aliyah is our calling and contribution to the great scheme of the *euangelion*.

Contrary to the dispensationalist view, there is a strong overarching suggestion that the salvation of most of the house of Israel will take place when the Jewish people return to the land (see F Wright, *Eschatology, Origins and Consequences*).

Ezekiel 36:16f gives a wonderful description of the process of salvation and sanctification when the Jewish people are returned to the land. This passage quite remarkably points out that in addition to the salvation taking place, the very act will sanctify the Lord's Holy Name before all nations. Hebrews 8:8-12 references Jeremiah 31, which speaks of a time after both the physical and spiritual restoration of Israel.

Of particular interest is Romans 11:25. The mystery is threefold: 1) A part of Israel is hardened for a limited amount of time, 2) the salvation of the Gentiles will precede the salvation of Israel and 3) all Israel will be saved.

It is important to state that CSA ministries do not, as is sometimes suggested, subscribe to dual covenant theology, the basic tenet of which is that, as Jewish people are party to the covenants, they do not need to make the Pauline shift in recognising Yeshua.

CSA ministries, as carrying agencies, are subject to the laws of Israel which forbid inducements – either financial or in kind – to persuade anyone to change his or her faith. Although we give out scripture sheets, we do not give out whole Bibles as these could be considered to be inducement in kind as they have monetary value.

But there have never been sanctions against sharing testimony or dialogue.

It is worth noting that the traditional methods of evangelisation towards Jewish people have been terribly flawed by de-Judaising elements and dispensationalism. In the 21st century, the traditional 'evangelical mugging' hardly works with Gentiles let alone Jewish people. It is generally considered that, according to the so-called Engle scale, it takes around ten encounters with the gospel before the possibility of commitment. For Jewish people, they probably don't start at zero anyway; more like minus ten in view of Christianity's history. In one sense it could be said that Jewish people, when in contact with Christians, are not as much interested in what you say as who you are and what you do.

The energy, time, commitment and warmth of those helping the Jewish people throughout the aliyah process, sometimes taking several years, is the most effective form of introducing them to their own Messiah!

Chapter 14

The Changing Face of Aliyah

When Christian-sponsored aliyah became a possibility and subsequently a reality, we had no real idea how effective it would be, or how long it would last. Even before the possibility arose following the publication of Steve Lightle's *Exodus II* in 1983, people had been preparing accommodation, transport, food and other supplies against a day in the future when it would become a reality. At the time of writing we are still in aliyah awaiting the day when it would become exodus. Those of us who have worked on aliyah from the earliest days believe that, whereas preparing for the future has its own merit, the emphasis should be on *now*.

Little did we think that thirty years later, in a very different world, we would still be working on aliyah strategies and that it would still be our all-consuming passion. However, the face of aliyah has changed over the years and by God's grace we are still tirelessly involved in the return of the Jewish people to their ancient homeland. The biggest challenge facing us today is to respond to the changes and plan, as far as possible, in an ever-changing world.

The flood to Israel of one million Russian-speaking immigrants that followed the fall of the Soviet Union in the 1990s gradually slowed down as the world situation changed and the number of potential immigrants from countries where Jews faced peril was assumed to have fallen. The early to middle 1990s was a period of undue optimism in world affairs and saw best-selling books such as Francis Fukayama's *The End of History* and similar publications, seeing the fall of Communism as the beginning of a new conflict-free era. So there was little or no increase in interest for aliyah from the rest of the diaspora with the exception of Ethiopia.

In 1990, Israel absorbed some 200,000 immigrants and throughout the 1990s an average of 75,000 immigrants came each year. The mass movement was known as 'push aliyah'. By 2008, which we may consider to be a pivotal year, the annual number had dropped to 15,452, according to the Jewish Agency, which handles immigration to Israel. Over the last five years, most immigrants were still from the former Soviet Republics, but numbers are increasing at greater rates than in previous years, especially from France and Belgium due to terrorist activities. Benjamin Netanyahu made a true but chilling comment in 2016 when he said that there was no future for the Jews of France.

In 2008 Jewish Agency chairman Nathan Sharansky shared with the Agency Assembly that 94% of Jews lived in countries with relative freedom and prosperity, with little need to leave these countries under duress or for lack of tolerance. Instead, the majority of the new olim were now making 'aliyah of choice' – a personal desire to be living in Israel at a unique and extraordinary time in its history. These olim had come with a different face than the waves of previous olim as they were not fleeing a totalitarian state or an economically devastated area. They were coming from a sense of pride, an aspiration for change, and an inspired sense of their Jewish self-identity. In short, they were coming to Israel because of who they are, not because of where they were domiciled.

Within seven years, the situation changed radically in some parts of the world due to the international financial crash, particularly in Latin America. In Europe, there is something akin to a pincer movement against the Jewish people being fuelled on the one hand by neo-Nazism, for example in Hungary, where Jobbik, the neo-Nazi party, have governmental positions. When questioned, 91% of more than 500 respondents said anti-Semitism has increased in the past five years. That figure was 88% in France, 87% in Belgium and 80% in Sweden. In Germany, Italy and Britain, some 60% of respondents identified a growth in anti-Semitism. Greece has a similar problem with the Nazi Golden

Dawn movement who are being trained by Greek Special Services. By the end of 2018, anti-Semitism in Europe and America was increasing at a staggering rate with France being deemed the worst place for Jewish people.

In addition, Islamic fundamentalism is the major tension in places like Belgium, France and Scandinavia. In Malmo, Sweden, physical attacks have fuelled a Jewish exodus. A generation ago, Malmo was home to 2,000 Jews; there are now fewer than 700 with anti-Semitic hate crimes in Sweden's third-largest city having almost tripled in recent years with no convictions.

Denmark's Jewish community has lost 25 percent of its registered members over the past 15 years, partly due to anti-Semitism, according to the Jewish community president. In an interview with Danish daily *Jillands-Posten*, Finn Schwarz said the community currently has 1,899 members compared to 2,639 in 1997. According to Denmark's cultural Jewish magazine *Goldberg*, "anti-Semitism is seen in verbal and physical threats, but also in the repeated discussions among politicians on banning circumcision and shechita, the religious ritual slaughter of animals".

According to an Anti-Defamation League report, many Europeans share classic anti-Semitic sentiments such as Jews having too much power in business. A poll revealed that 73% of Hungarians, 60% in Spain, 54% of Poles, 39% of Italians, 35% of French, 30% of Austrians, 22% of Germans, 21% of Norwegians and 20% of British respondents believe the statement that "Jews have too much power in business".

The statement "Jews are more loyal to Israel than to the country of their residence" was seen as "likely correct" by 72% of the Spanish, 61% of Italians and Poles, 58% of Norwegians, 55% of Hungarians and Germans, 48% of the British, 47% of Austrians and the Dutch, and 45% of the French.

The statement that the Jews still talk too much about what happened to them during the Holocaust was found to be held by 63% of Hungarians, 53% of Poles, 48% of Italians, 47% in Spain,

45% of Austrians, 43% of Germans, 35% in France, 31% in Holland, 25% of Norwegians and 24% of British respondents. The idea that the Jews and the State of Israel capitalise on the Holocaust, and have turned it into a massive industry, is a widespread libel.

The tactics employed by the BDS movement, along with the ongoing efforts by anti-Israel student groups seeking to stifle discourse about the Israeli-Palestinian conflict and Israel in general, through disruption and defamation, is a deeply troubling phenomenon. BDS has contributed to an atmosphere at some institutions where Jewish and pro-Israel students feel uncomfortable voicing their views or even asserting their Jewish identity.

An effect of the rise of blatant anti-Semitism is that many Jewish people are reluctant to appear in public places wearing anything that defines them as being Jewish. In France, 40% said they avoided wearing such items in public, followed by Belgium with 36%. In addition, 22% said they no longer visited or attended advertised Jewish events. Schools and Jewish social centres in France and Belgium are generally located on first floors with bomb doors as entrances and security personnel guarding the buildings.

In France, a woman was arrested in Toulouse after trying to stab a student at a Jewish day school where four Jews were shot and killed in March 2012. In addition, a Jewish-owned pharmacy in Paris was destroyed by youths protesting Israel's military campaign in Gaza while the Charlie Hebdo and Kosher market atrocities along with the Bataclan massacre and associated attacks are still fresh in the memory and led to Benjamin Netanyahu calling Jewish people not only to leave France but all of Western Europe as well. Olim numbers are currently rising, but many French Jews are unable to leave due to documentation problems, especially those from Algeria. Many others still are so secularised that they do not self-identify as being Jewish. Ezra are working with a newly-formed network to help facilitate and prepare Jewish people for aliyah.

At the time I began writing this account it was hard to imagine that the changes in Ukraine could be so dangerous to the 400,000 Jewish people who still live there. It all started with the small demonstration of students who protested the decision of the Ukrainian government not to sign an agreement with the European Union. The demonstration was brutally dispersed by the special police unit. As a result, many students were hospitalised with multiple fractures and head injuries.

Thousands, and later hundreds of thousands, of Ukrainian people rebelled against the blatant excessive use of force employed. They all gathered in Kiev's central square and set up street camps on the main street and surrounding areas. Later, large groups of radical nationalists came to Kiev from the Western Ukraine and many residents provided them with food, shelter, clothes, firewood and money.

In the course of time, the situation grew into a full-scale protest against the present government and President Viktor Yanukovich, who began to cruelly suppress the protests by employing police forces from the whole of Ukraine, including Speznaz, the special forces unit. Firearms were commonly employed and, as a result, five people died – according to the official news agency, twenty-eight are still missing.

A direct consequence of the disturbances was an overt expression of antagonism towards the Jews with vitriolic language and wild accusations against them from both sides. A common charge was that the Jews committed the murders of those who died whilst demonstrations were being dispersed as there are Jews in the Ukrainian government.

The largest department store on the main street of Kiev was undergoing exterior renovations and the big windows were boarded up. There the age-old conspiracy theory re-emerged when a slogan was spray-painted across them, 'Blame the Jews, not the Government!'

In several regions of the Ukraine the representatives of Orthodox churches began to distribute leaflets which call upon people to take up arms and punish the Jews who want to separate and destroy Ukraine and all that it means.

A Kiev resident, Dov Baar Glickman, was viciously attacked by three assailants, who knocked him to the ground and stabbed him multiple times. He managed to drag himself to a nearby ritual bath and was taken from there to hospital, Israel Radio reported. The attack on Glickman was the second against Jews in Kiev in recent days. A couple of days earlier four men ambushed Israeli-born Hebrew teacher Hillel Wertheimer at his apartment building after following him home from synagogue services, according to Joseph Zissels, a vice-president of the World Jewish Congress.

Rabbi Pinchas Goldschmidt, president of the Conference of European Rabbis, said tolerance of anti-Semitic statements by the Ukrainian government and the Opposition gave anti-Semites free reign to attack Jews. He called on the government to protect Ukrainian Jews and decisively quash anti-Semitism.

US-born Rabbi Yaakov Bleich said the two attacks were complicating an already complex situation for Kiev's 70,000 Jews, who have been frightened by the attacks, some keeping their children home from shul and yeshiva, causing the rabbi to hire a consortium of security companies, at a cost of $25,000 a month, to calm fears and keep life flowing as smoothly as possible.

Even news of the resignation of Prime Minister Mykola Azarov did not ease the community's concerns. Rabbi Bleich said: 'We are not loosening up on our security. Until these guys are found we are still, unfortunately, a target.'

Viktor, an Ezra field worker, added: 'The police do not actively respond to any complaints and turn a blind eye as some are connected with gangster bands and, together with them, agitate against the Jews. For this reason, nobody relies on them.'

In October last year Jewish businessman Dmitry Flekman, 28, told the Jewish Telegraph Agency and other media he was tortured and beaten by police officers from the city of Lviv in western Ukraine because he was Jewish.

The situation has encouraged many Jews to think again about leaving for Israel. The Ezra offices there immediately began to receive double the usual number of calls, most needing help with information, documentation, transportation and financial assistance.

The annexation of the Crimea caused untold misery for both national Ukrainians and the Jewish people, with Jews once again blamed for the troubles. There are four defining factors of anti-Semitism in Europe:

Firstly, European officials remain reluctant to identify the ideological or religious motivations of the perpetrators. Secondly, surveys show that negative attitudes towards Jews among Europe's population remain widespread. Thirdly, these surveys confirm that some of this bias reveals itself through certain criticisms of the state of Israel. Finally, a number of European governments and political parties have added fuel to the fire by backing restrictions on vital religious practices. At least four countries – Iceland, Norway, Sweden and Switzerland – ban kosher slaughter. Authorities and political forces in Norway, Denmark and Germany have also tried to ban infant male circumcision. Whereas these restrictions also affect Muslims, they are generally considered to be Jewish practices.

In the USA, there are elements of both vulgar and racist anti-Semitism in addition to anti-Israelism which pollutes both church and society. There has never been a large-scale aliyah movement in the USA but it is rising. However, the number of Jewish people going to the States still outnumbers those leaving. They are referred to as *yordim* (those who go down). CSA in the USA generally operates by sponsoring flights.

Meanwhile an increasing number of people who had not paid too much attention to their Jewish heritage are looking for a way back. Examples are in Portugal, Spain and elsewhere. These include the B'nei Anousim (Marranos), descendants of those forced to convert under the Inquisition, the B'nei Menashe (descended from the tribe of Menashe, also forced to convert) and the hidden Jews of Poland and other former Nazi-controlled areas. Also among these are the children and grandchildren of those placed up for adoption during the war and generally raised as Catholics. The JA response is [that]:

'These people are no longer halachically Jewish, but they fall under the category of *zera Yisrael,* part of the extended Jewish family – we need to be there for them.' It is envisioned that a similar process would be applied to them as to the *Falash Mura* forcibly converted Ethiopian Jews and their descendants who were received into the land on condition they underwent immediate conversion procedures upon arrival.

The increase in European aliyah has brought some changes in Israel where a greater use of English in governmental initiatives and business practices has emerged. The problem of incoming olim from Europe and the USA is changing some dimensions in industry and commerce.

One significant factor, particularly in the USA, is that many Jewish people, and particularly the Orthodox, lead a reasonably sheltered life, and most enjoy an affluent lifestyle and see no reason to make aliyah, although some will buy property in Israel as a gesture. Among the Chasidim, there is a tradition that aliyah is the Messiah's task and aliyah can only happen when Messiah arrives.

Outside the former Soviet bloc, as in Europe before the Holocaust, there remains a certain reluctance to believe that things will get worse, and many are reluctant to leave locations where they have put down roots, live an affluent life or have 'married out' and become secularised.

The days of 'push aliyah' finished a few years ago and the traditional fishing methods associated with this have needed to be revisited. In the fSU, there were a disenfranchised, powerless people living in abject poverty, having no sense of Jewish history or culture. By showing the love of the Lord and helping them in all manner of ways by providing food, clothing and medicine in addition to the practical processing, the aliyah in some senses generally found a receptive client group.

As soon as the 'gates opened', the Lubavich Chabad mounted a large-scale initiative to reclaim synagogues such as the one in Kiev that had been confiscated and turned into a puppet theatre, and provide them with a rabbi. The idea was to ensure every city and major historical Jewish centre had a synagogue and rabbi. Some of the earlier religious leaders were quite friendly but, by and large, as the years passed and the programme began to gather pace, a two-fold tension developed in which both local authorities and Jewish religious authorities made things difficult for aliyah. As we have seen, some of the major Chassidic houses see aliyah as a theological aberration, to the extent that, during the war, some saw the Holocaust as God's punishment for the sin of Zionism. The general position of some Chassidim has been that, while not teaching against aliyah, they do not encourage it; the feeling being that Jews should stay where they are and rebuild the historic Jewish communities until Messiah arrives to lead them back to the promised land.

A further tension is that Jewish history, as taught by the influx of Lubavitch and others, has focused a great deal on Christian anti-Semitism and caused a certain level of suspicion to arise as to the motives of CSA.

New approaches are needed, ranging from the biblical to the intellectual, encouraging the reclaiming and renewing of Jewish identity with more emphasis on the beauty and opportunities available within the land both from a physical and spiritual point of view.

We need to seek the Lord diligently as to how we can best serve the Jewish people in a changing world. We have tried all along, across the CSA ministries, to sanctify the Lord's name through aliyah, but we are all aware that the times are in the Lord's hand. Twenty-seven years have passed – maybe a lot longer than many of us thought at the outset. We may have responded to the immediate needs from 1989. I feel in one sense that we have scratched the surface and enjoyed the excitement and blessings of *push aliyah*, but the pincer movements of neo-fascism and nationalism, along with Jihadist Islam, pose a worldwide threat to the Jewish people that may need another immediate response. Pray that we will be prepared.

Chapter 15

The Changing Face of Aliya II
The Rise of Vladimir Putin

Vladimir Putin has enjoyed a spectacular rise to power under various titles: Acting President (1999–2000); First Presidential term (2000–2004); Second Presidential term (2004–2008); Second Premiership (2008–2012). He was barred from a third term by the constitution, with First Deputy Prime Minister Dmitry Medvedev elected his successor. But, in a power-switching operation on 8th May 2008, only a day after handing the presidency to Medvedev, Putin was appointed Prime Minister of Russia, maintaining his political dominance. On 4th March 2012, he won the 2012 Russian presidential elections in the first round with 63.6% of the vote.

A former Lieutenant-Colonel in the KGB, its surrogates and successors, Putin has basically defaulted to the pre-Communist Russian ideal of autocracy, nationalism and orthodoxy, a triple standard that has rendered Russian history different from all others with the exception of a few years in Spain in the late fifteenth century (See F Wright, *Within the Pale*, 2004).

Autocracy

We need not detain ourselves here as the opening paragraph illustrated the situation. It is well known that all opposition to Putin is not tolerated and has been ruthlessly put down at great cost.

Nationalism

Although the presidential flag was introduced under Boris Yeltsin, it was seldom used whereas today it is not only used in formal and ceremonial settings but frequently in place of the national flag. Under Putin, Russia has progressively become the subject of rising xenophobia and nationalism, with nationalist demonstrations and riots becoming commonplace. The deployment of the ultra-nationalist biker gang, the *Night Wolves*, numbering over 5,000 members, has often been used as a tool of enforcement.

This group is led by the towering figure of Alexander Zaldostanov, also known as *The Surgeon*, who has often been pictured with Putin, usually while riding side by side on Harley Davidson motorcycles. In 2015 they planned a 3,728-mile long ride lasting two weeks, passing through Belarus, Poland, the Czech Republic, Slovakia and Austria before finishing in Berlin. It was intended as a World War II memorial, but the overtone was that these are some of the lands Putin wants returned to a powerful new Russian empire.

Putin has denied this or at least distanced himself from ambitions to 'reunite' Moldova, the Ukraine (in total), Poland, Czech Republic, Slovakia, Romania and the Baltics (Latvia, Lithuania and Estonia) to 'Mother Russia'. Crimea and Belarus by default are already there, and the eastern republics are in process.

Following the traditional pattern of European nationalism, no matter which group is the current focus of animus – whether migrant workers, African soccer players or gays – it soon enough falls to the Jews to be presented as the primary source of all misfortune.

A particularly worrying element is linking Jews with facilitating gays in their practices, and the production of gay porn movies and literature. A gay rights leader in Moscow has been saturating the internet, Facebook and Twitter with these vile defamations, with Putin's apparent blessing. Needless to say, the notion has been picked up by nationalist movements in other parts of Europe.

Following the 2014 Ukrainian revolution, Russian occupation of Crimea was undertaken because 'Crimea has always been and remains an inseparable part of Russia', according to Putin. After Russia's annexation, he said that Ukraine includes 'regions of Russia's historic south' and 'was created on a whim by the Bolsheviks'. He went on to declare that the February 2014 ousting of Ukrainian President Viktor Yanukovych had been orchestrated by the West as an attempt to weaken Russia. 'Our Western partners have crossed a line. They behaved rudely, irresponsibly and unprofessionally,' he said, adding that those who had come to power in Ukraine were 'nationalists, neo-Nazis, Russophobes and anti-Semites'. In a July 2014 speech amidst an armed insurgency in Eastern Ukraine, Putin said he would use Russia's entire arsenal and the right of self-defence to protect Russian speakers outside Russia. In late August 2014, he said, 'People who have their own views on history and the history of our country may argue with me, but it seems to me that the Russian and Ukrainian peoples are practically one people.' Nationalism is clearly seen in the above, but the subtler element and agent of anti-Semitism is Orthodoxy.

Orthodoxy

The position of the Orthodox Church during Communism was at best ambiguous. Although effectively outlawed, it was still mildly tolerated in some areas. Recently released archives suggest that past and current leaders of the church were, by and large, KGB agents, but the leak was quickly suppressed.

The Russian Orthodox Church outlasted the official atheism of the Soviet Union and now, under Putin, has regained most of the power it exercised under the Romanoffs, being influential in all spheres of life.

Vladimir Putin is unusual in that he was baptised in secret as a child. He personally oversaw the resurrection of the Russian Orthodox Church including the reconstruction of some 23,000 churches destroyed or fallen into disuse during the years of communism.

Both the Kremlin and the Church have benefited from resuming their centuries-old alliance. Early in Putin's rule, a law was passed returning all church property seized during the Soviet era, which almost surely makes the Moscow Patriarchate the largest landowner in Russia. State-owned energy companies have contributed billions of rubles to the reconstruction of churches around the country, in particular the beautification of the external structures. Putin has encouraged the presence of the church as a bastion of patriotism, and around 90% of Russians consider themselves part of the church even though some openly say they have no real faith. It has, however, become the litmus test of patriotism and loyalty.

The influence of the Orthodox position as part of national identity has led to a groundswell of the traditional anti-Semitism with all its attendant vulgar motifs. Whereas a few short years ago it was considered that Russian aliyah had more or less come to an end, in some areas it has now experienced a significant upsurge.

The Baltics

Many were horrified in early May 2015 by Putin's defence of the 1939 Molotov-Ribbentrop Pact between Hitler and Stalin allies which opened the way to World War II. The deal effectively allowed the Soviet Union to occupy Estonia, Latvia and Lithuania, portions of Poland and Bessarabia for half-a-century. A more disturbing fact is that the Kremlin are once again thinking about 'a preventative occupation' of the Baltic countries, a step that could trigger the collapse of parts of northern Europe and NATO, or even a third world war.

Moreover, as in 1939, Moscow's duplicity and cynicism about such an initiative taken in the name of improving its defence capability is, in reality, a potential measure to advance Russian imperialism and bring disorder and confusion to the Western powers.

A telling article by Moscow commentator Rostislav Ishchenko called for a 'preventive' strike against the Baltic littoral (coastline) in order to block what he sees as a threat from NATO. According to Ishchenko, Moscow has a number of compelling reasons to launch occupation of at least portions of the Baltic countries in order to counter NATO, even if there is no such threat in real terms. Further, that such a measure is needed in order to extend a land corridor to the [potentially] blockaded group of forces in Kaliningrad (an autonomous Russian area sandwiched between

Poland and Lithuania). In addition, such a measure is needed to free up forces for actions in other more important directions.

Ishchenko further suggests that 'the main goal of this operation would be not the defence of [Russia's] borders from imagined enemies, but the occasion for beginning trade with Europe over borders and spheres of influence. Needless to say, the sovereignty of other countries and the will of the peoples living in them are not, and cannot, be taken into any kind of consideration.'

Strategically, such an action makes good sense as Paris and Berlin could not 'fight' for the Baltic countries if they no longer existed.

Whereas it would be comforting to think Ishchenko's article is simply an example of the journalistic political rabble-rousing that often arises in countries during times of power surges, sadly this is not the case.

Aleksander Sytin, a former analyst for Russia's *SVR* intelligence service and the now infamous Russian Institute for Strategic Research, currently working closely with *Russia Today* and other Kremlin media outlets, argues that Ishchenko is speaking for more than himself. Sytin believes the article has the simultaneous intention of testing the waters of public opinion and expanding the limits of what people consider permissible. Moscow wants to see this kind of thought spread through the population so that the regime can act nominally in the name of 'the will of the people', even though the source of the ideas is the Kremlin itself.

Sytin's final comment was that the Kremlin's current aggression is creating a danger much greater than that which came from 'the evil empire' operating under the name USSR.

In conclusion, the situation for the Jewish people in Putin's domain and anticipated domains is moving towards a return of *push aliyah* in these areas before it is too late. It has already begun. It is a sad fact of history and present-day reality that Jewish people will be blamed for whatever troubling events result from these Russian incursions.

In March 2014, Rabbi Mikhail Kapustin of Simferopol was forced to flee Crimea after denouncing Russian actions. His synagogue was defaced by a swastika and, a month later, vandals defaced Sevastopol's monument to 4,200 Jews murdered by the Nazis in July 1942. Tensions remain high but there is still some movement of Jewish people to Israel.

At the time of going to press, Putin is gradually enacting a series of edicts that deny most expressions of Christianity as well as 'other religions' outside of the Orthodox Church. From 20th July 2016 religious meetings in homes, via the media or in non-recognised premises (read non-Orthodox Churches) were banned forthwith. The measures are classed as anti-terrorist and national security issues!

Chapter 16

Those Who Cannot Make Aliyah

In common with most involved in CSA, hardly a thought was given to those who could not make aliyah, for a variety of reasons. On reflection, I suppose we were so busy with the 'push' it didn't really arise. We generally thought those who were not making aliyah at any given moment would make it later, or had simply denied their own place within the movement.

The major reasons why some cannot make aliyah were, and remain, involved with documentation and government policies both in Ukraine and Israel. At the turn of the century there was a policy to end indirect absorption which in essence meant that in certain cases such as the elderly, infirm or sick, if they had no-one to go to, their aliyah opportunities became severely limited.

Secondly, if you had any debt, particularly to the government (in Ukrainian cities all the utilities including the telephone are paid to the government apparatus), you were not allowed to leave. If you worked in the public services, other than the police, wages were paid infrequently, if at all, and pensions were insufficient to cover monthly outgoings.

Thirdly, if you had living parents you had to have their permission to leave. Pensions are so low that it effectively means the children have to take on responsibility to care for parents. The issue is troublesome as many do not even know if their parents are alive. Many who were soldiers never came back from Afghanistan and other theatres of operation, yet are not listed as dead, while marriages fall apart and one parent may well leave home, never to be heard from again. Children are brought up by relatives, and one or other parent may well go missing. So no permission to leave can be granted.

It was about the turn of the century when we were all worrying about Y2K that I awoke with a start and felt the Lord impressing on me that we had made second class citizens out of those who could not make aliyah. I wasn't sure how to approach such a challenge but felt chastened within.

I managed to get the remaining ex-members of the dance team together with a couple of their friends who had a heart for the Jewish people and arranged to meet them all in Kiev at the apartment of one our former lady bus drivers. The apartment overlooked the synagogue and the statue of Sholem Aleichem.

We gathered together and prayed to seek the Lord's will for the new work and felt we could start with one full-time worker to investigate the possibilities and liaise with the appropriate Jewish authorities. Inga, a dear friend and previous co-worker who had led the dance team, was the one I had hoped would start the work, but as her husband had just been appointed pastor of a church in Kharkov she felt she needed to support him. In the event, on her recommendation, another young lady took up the position with a couple of others as volunteers and we embarked upon a new venture, starting in Kiev. Chesed International Ministries (Messianic Chesed in Ukraine) was born.

Initially, we started by simply getting lists of needy people from the JA and Jewish community leaders. The approach was simple – knock on the door and ask if the people had any needs. We had seen a great deal of poverty on fishing expeditions but what we found in some of the city's tower blocks was appalling. The entrances were often squalid and smelt of urine and stale tobacco. Initially, the first tasks undertaken were doing the washing, cleaning the flats and repairing the so-called plumbing. As trust developed, we began doing the shopping, taking them to doctors and hospitals and picking up prescriptions.

One event that added a new dimension to the ministry and from which point the work spread to Donetsk, Dnepropetrovsk and Kharkov, was being invited to visit an elderly couple. The walls of their dilapidated flat were covered in theatre posters of them when they were professional musicians and singers, including certificates for performing for the Politburo. Amidst abject poverty, the room reeked of urine. The lady had senile dementia and her husband, who loved her dearly, had not been out of the apartment for three years in order to be able to look after her the best he could with no help or money. He used to play guitar and sing some of their old songs to her, and occasionally she would return a small smile. We cleaned the flat from top to bottom, fixed the leaky taps, repainted it and bought sets of bedding, incontinence pads and medication for sores, and one of our girls started twice-daily visits and stayed over twice a week so the husband could go out. When she died a few months later, he was in tears as he thanked us for allowing his wife to die with dignity in a clean bed. We were very moved by this and, from that point, care of the dying became a feature of the ministry to those Jewish people who could not make aliyah.

On one occasion Inga was in a mostly rural village where she had an encounter with a lady who used to walk the streets screaming and shouting and, although not violent, was very threatening and at times aggressive. Inga felt compassion and approached her asking if she could help. The lady told her in an extremely agitated state that no-one could help. The doctors could not help, the rabbi could not help, and there was no help from God. Inga asked her why and she responded that during the Great Patriotic War she had been an abortionist in the Red Army and had carried out over 2,000 abortions. She could not sleep because all she could see were the countless faces of those lives she had ended, and thereupon fell into a screaming fit. Inga quietly asked a group of bystanders if this was in fact the case, and they affirmed that she had been in the Red Army Medical Corps and had indeed been employed in such a manner. Inga quietly comforted her and rebuked the evil spirit. The lady calmed down and Inga told her that there was forgiveness through Messiah. They quietly prayed together and the lady was immediately restored to her normal mind after many years. The onlookers were so astounded they fell to the ground to seek their own redemption. We refurbished her tiny home and restored the water supply. She has never had a relapse and went on to live a happy normal life and became an enthusiastic member of the Bible study group as she awaited the aliyah process. Sadly, she died before the process was completed but did so in peace, with the love of Messiah in her heart.

Hitler's war against the Jews was fought on two different fronts. In the West, during the early stages of the persecution, Jewish people were rounded up and became subject to a series of passive methods of extermination. Deprivation of the means of raising income and primary healthcare combined with excessively hard labour, malnutrition and medical experiments under the guise of treatment, were all employed.

But in the eastern campaign the Nazis showed no such restraints. Mobile killing squads known as Einsatzgruppen, under the auspices of the Reich Security Main Office (RHSA) commanded by Rheinhard Heidrich, swept through Eastern Europe, exterminating the Jewish communities *en masse* as they pressed forward. There were four such groups designated A, B, C and D made up of SS officers, members of the Wehrmacht, local militia, Nazis and 'patriots', each unit numbering around 800 persons. In the Ukraine, Belarus and Russia the local nationalists would often greet the incoming Einsatzgruppen with a pile of dead Jewish bodies as a welcome present. The most notorious such atrocity took place on the outskirts of Kiev at Babi Yar where two small detachments of the 'C' unit massacred 37,771 men, women and children, shot in a little under thirty-six hours. The local people welcomed the Germans with acclaim and cooperation. A local militia had been set up and became heavily involved in the spectacle which was attended by local people with approval and regarded as entertaining.

There were many other instances. One of the lesser known took place at Drobritsky Yar outside Kharkov during the Christmas and

New Year period of 1941-42. We encountered a few survivors during the bussing programme and later helped a few through Chesed. The following is the story related to us over an afternoon cup of tea by survivors Elena and her childhood friend Yevgeny who were respectively eleven and nine years old at the time.

Elena was a bright child living in the Dershinsky area of Kharkov with her parents Isaly and Razaylya and her three-year-old sister. On 25th October the German Army arrived in Kharkov, one of the furthest points reached in their penetration of the USSR. Immediately a local militia emerged and set about appropriating all available food supplies by confiscation. Random killing and executions of Jewish people and others designated undesirable became commonplace. As the first weeks progressed, only those collaborating with the Germans were able to sustain themselves.

In common with usual practice, the Germans immediately took a census of nationality and registered 10,271 Jewish people. The figure was lower than reality as not all Jewish people registered themselves as Jewish. Those who were half-Jewish registered in their mother's maiden name if their father was Jewish. The use of either parent's surname was and remained a fairly common practice through to the 1990s.

With their usual ruthless determination, the Nazis soon upped the total through bribes, sanctions and investigation. On 14th December notices were posted by the town commandant – in the Russian, Ukrainian and German languages – that all Jewish people, those of Jewish descent, and those married to Jews, were to report to the tractor factory in the Drobritsky Yar area within 48 hours.

The people were informed that this was to be a temporary arrangement prior to resettlement and work. Many had heard reports of ghettoisation in other areas and assumed this was going to be a similar exercise. Those who were physically unable to make the 16km trek in the freezing cold were summarily executed. A horrified Elena saw her wheelchair-bound father shot in the head before her eyes.

As Jews clutching a few wretched possessions were marched to the factory, accompanied by whips and dogs to keep them going, any lagging or showing signs of exhaustion were instantly shot. They had hardly begun the trek when their homes were systematically looted by the locals. Upon arrival on 16th December, they were herded into factory units with no windows and only one door which was kept locked. No bedding, sanitation, heating or water was available and only meagre food was provided.

Unlike the other mass executions in Kiev and Odessa, the Nazis were concerned by the proximity of the fast-approaching Red Army who were expected in the opening days of the New Year. On Christmas Day, the Nazis informed the people that due to overcrowding and supply problems they would be moved in medium-sized units to nearby villages and towns to start a new life. The grim reality was that groups of between two and three hundred at a time were driven the short distance to the nearby ravine where they were either neck shot or machine-gunned. At least 16,000 men, women and children lost their lives between Christmas and New Year in what became named 'Hitler's Christmas Present'. Reflecting the apparent urgency of the action, the general practice of stripping their victims naked and sending their clothes and possessions back to Germany was abandoned in that they were shot fully clothed.

In common with most other *aktions* by the Einsatzgruppen and local militias, not all were killed outright; many were thrown into the pits wounded along with some who were simply buried alive. Some managed to crawl to the edges of the pits before the area was either burned or undermined. On completion of the grisly task, all the carefully completed documents were burned and the factory destroyed. When the Red Army passed through, a special *Kommando* was sent to Drobritsky Yar to exhume the bodies and burn them to destroy evidence of the atrocity.

Because of the hurried way this was carried out, it seems that some of the usual exterminatory procedures were not adhered to as rigidly as in other locations. Yevgeny's mother, who was Jewish and a doctor, also perished. But his father, who was Russian, and by default himself, were told shortly after arrival at the factory to leave immediately or be shot. They both survived, living a meagre existence until the end of the war, constantly avoiding anti-Semitic elements on both sides.

In the confusion during the loading of the lorries to the ravine, Elena and her mother managed to escape, but the younger sister had sadly died in the factory. They were found by partisans and, despite being Jewish, were treated kindly and survived the war. When, in 1993, I first met Elena and her mother along with some of the other handful of survivors, they said that they had to be very careful how they spoke. The city was still subject to tensions between those who served or collaborated with the Nazis and those who fought with the Red Army. If anyone spoke out of turn about the events, there was a real chance of reprisals from both sides. This tension could be found in many parts of the Ukraine in the early days.

At the time of our visit, the site was marked by a three-foot high memorial covered with cheap, peeling pale blue paint. Some ten years later a new memorial and small museum were constructed. In the early 1990s there was a regular bus run from Kharkov and a good number of Jewish people left for Israel. Of those who lived through the Holocaust, Chesed had the privilege of caring for a good number and tended to them in their last hours. One of our Chesed workers, Svetlana, had a wonderful gift of caring for the housebound and the dying.

One of these was Lena. Ironically, she was a well-respected doctor who had specialised in geriatrics, as we call it in the West. But as she reached retirement age, her husband, a leading surgeon, died. Pensions in the fSU and Ukraine did not reflect status and profession. She had been involved in a road traffic accident while arranging her husband's funeral that subsequently rendered her unable to walk. In our terms, because she was a widow and had no children, she was abandoned. The meagre state pension was all she had to live on and she was confined to her apartment on the third floor. It is hard for us in the West to comprehend how a woman of this calibre could be reduced to this state. But it's still not uncommon in the fSU.

A similar case was in Belarus where two leading academics from the University of Minsk were impoverished on their retirement during the last days of communism. In an attempt to subdue intellectuals, a tractor driver was paid more than a university professor, but the academics did get better state accommodation. We had the privilege of helping this dear couple make their aliyah in 1991 after spending several early morning breakfasts with them.

I also had the privilege of visiting Lena before we arranged her aliyah. Although unable to get off her bed until we helped her, she was still helping her former patients and their relatives by telephone. A very refined and cultured lady, she bore her disability with grace and dignity. Whilst indisposed, with time on her hands, she was also trying to discover her Jewish identity and understand what it meant – not only for herself, but also for others. After our visits and spending time poring over the scriptures with her, she commenced a Bible study in her flat that attracted a good number of people. Eventually the number grew so large that they had to a find a bigger venue and transport Lena to the meetings. This thrilled her and I personally believe it helped enormously with her improvement in mobility and self-confidence post-accident. With our help, she gained a measure of mobility. Before she made her own aliyah, she had attracted many who would not only discover their Jewish identity but subsequently follow her to a new life in the land.

Afterword

The last year has seen a shocking rise in anti-Semitism in the UK, USA, France, Belgium, Netherlands, Germany, Bulgaria and Latin America in particular. Desecrations of graveyards, attacks on Jewish people including the beating of the Chief Rabbi of Argentina and his wife, have become commonplace. In the UK, institutional anti-Semitism has almost become a *de facto* element of Momentum, the group currently dominating the Labour Party, which was at one time regarded as the natural political home for Jewish people. Shadow Chancellor John McDonnell even went as far as to say that UK nationals who have served in the IDF should be stripped of their citizenship whilst at the same time lobbying for Daesh fighters to be brought home, thus retaining their citizenship – a move applauded by Diane Abbott, Shadow Home Secretary. Labour leader Jeremy Corbyn himself has a record of supporting anti-Semitic, terrorist groups as is common knowledge.

A poll commissioned by Cable News Network (CNN) revealed the following horrific data. More than a quarter of Europeans believe Jews have too much influence in business and finance while nearly one in four said Jews have too much influence in conflict and wars across the world. One in five said they have too much influence in the media and the same number believe they have too much influence in politics.

Meanwhile a third of the Europeans polled said they knew just a little or nothing at all about the Holocaust – the mass murder of six million Jews in lands controlled by Adolf Hitler's Nazi regime in the 1930s and 1940s. The figure increases with Canadians and Californians, being largely ignorant about the Holocaust, reaching as high as 60% in younger people. The Anti-Defamation League report that, after taking a worldwide poll in 2014/15, a conservative estimate of people holding anti-Semitic views numbers 1.09 billion, with mainland Europe and the fSU being the major culprits. The number has increased since then. It is generally considered that anti-Semitism is higher now than any time following the Holocaust. Turkey had the highest score with 72%. Euronews reports that anti-Semitic incidents in France rose by a staggering 68% in 2018 with the figure even higher at the time of going to press. According to a recent BBC programme, France is now rated the most anti-Semitic country in Europe. Several hundred Jews questioned by the EU's Fundamental Rights Agency said they had experienced a physical, anti-Semitic attack in the past year while 28% said they had been harassed. The survey showed that 89% of the 16,395 Jews surveyed considered online anti-Semitism a problem in their country while 2% were physically attacked. At least 47% worry about anti-Semitic verbal insult or harassment and 40% about physical attack in the next 12 months. Some 34% have avoided Jewish events at least occasionally because of safety fears and 38% have considered emigrating in the past five years over safety fears. A startling 95% of French Jews see anti-Semitism as either a fairly or very big problem. France has been subject to a string of jihadist attacks including the killing of hostages at a Jewish supermarket in Paris. Last year 85-year-old Holocaust survivor Mireille Knoll was murdered in her Paris flat and an eight-year-old boy wearing a kippah (skullcap) was attacked in the street by teenagers.

Please join with us in supporting CSA. Every Jewish life is precious and let us remember the following:

He who saves a life, it is if he saved the world. (Talmud)

They were pleased to do it, and indeed they owe it to them. For if the Gentiles have shared in their spiritual blessings, they are obligated to minister to them with material blessings (Rom 15:27).

Appendix 1

The great preacher Charles Haddon Spurgeon had a good understanding of the Lord's heart for Israel and the Jewish people. Following are a few extracts from his teaching –

A sermon delivered on June 3rd 1855 at the New Park Street Chapel, Southwark:

I think we do not attach sufficient importance to the restoration of the Jews. We do not think enough about it. But certainly, if there is anything promised in the Bible it is this. I imagine that you cannot read the Bible without seeing clearly that there is to be an actual restoration of the children of Israel... For when the Jews are restored, the fullness of the Gentiles shall be gathered in; and as soon as they return, then Jesus will come upon Mount Zion with His ancients gloriously, and the halcyon days of the millennium shall then dawn; we shall then know every man to be a brother and a friend; Christ shall rule with universal sway.

A sermon delivered at the Metropolitan Tabernacle on June 16th 1864 on The Restoration and Conversion of the Jews:

There will be a native government again; there will again be the form of a body politic; a state shall be incorporated, and a king shall reign. Israel has now become alienated from her own land. Her sons, though they can never forget the sacred dust of Palestine, yet die at a hopeless distance from her consecrated shores. But it shall not be so forever, for her sons shall again rejoice in her: her land shall be called Beulah, for as a young man marrieth a virgin, so shall her sons marry her. "I will place you in your own land" is God's promise to them... They are to have a national prosperity which shall make them famous; nay, so glorious shall they be that Egypt and Tyre and Greece and Rome shall all forget their glory in the greater splendour of the throne of David... If there be anything clear and plain, the literal sense and meaning of this passage [Ezekiel 37:1-10] – a meaning not to be spirited or spiritualised away – must be evident that both the two and the ten tribes of Israel are to be restored to their own land, and that a king is to rule over them.

'Once a Curse, But Now a Blessing' delivered on December 6th 1863 at the Metropolitan Tabernacle, Newington:

But the day is coming, yea it dawns already, when the whole world shall discern the true dignity of the chosen seed, and shall seek their company, because the Lord hath blessed them. In that day, when Israel shall look upon him whom they have pierced, and shall mourn for their sins, the Jew shall take his true rank among the nations as an elder brother and a prince. The covenant made with Abraham, to bless all nations by his seed, is not revoked; heaven and earth shall pass away, but the chosen nation shall not be blotted out from the book of remembrance. The Lord hath not cast away his people; he has never given their mother a bill of divorcement; he has never put them away; in a little wrath he hath hidden his face from them, but with great mercies will he gather them. The natural branches shall again be engrafted into the olive together with the wild olive graftings from among the Gentiles. In the Jew, first and chiefly, shall grace triumph through the King of the Jews. O time, fly thou with rapid wing, and bring the auspicious day.

Appendix 2

EARLY HYMNS RELATING TO THE RETURN

In his Short Hymns on Select Passages of the Holy Scriptures, published in 1762, Charles Wesley included the following hymn based on Isaiah 66:19, 20 and Romans 11:26. John Wesley selected it for his, *A Collection of Hymns for the Use of the People called Methodists*, published in 1780. Its significance lies in the way Charles Wesley looks forward to a restoration of Israel, and how from His re-gathered people, the gospel will be spread to all the nations. Here is the full text of the hymn:
(Usually sung to the tune of Crown Him with Many Crowns)

Almighty God of Love
Set up the attracting sign
And summon whom Thou dost approve
For messengers divine.
From Abram's favoured seed
Thy new apostles choose
In isles and continents to spread
The dead-reviving news.

Them snatched out of the flame
Through every nation send
The true Messiah to proclaim
The universal Friend.
That all the God unknown
May learn of Jews to adore
And see Thy glory in Thy Son
Till time shall be no more.

O that the chosen band
Might now their brethren bring
And gathered out of every land
Present to Zion's King.
Of all the ancient race
Not one be left behind
But each impelled by secret grace
His way to Canaan find

We know it must be done
For God hath spoke the word
All Israel shall their Saviour own
To their first state restored.
Rebuilt by His command
Jerusalem shall rise
Her temple on Moriah stand
Again, and touch the skies

Send then Thy servants forth
To call the Hebrews home
From west and east, and south, and north
Let all the wanderers come.
Where'er in lands unknown
Thy fugitives remain
Bid every creature help them on
Thy holy mount to gain.

An offering to their God
There let them all be seen
Sprinkled with water and with blood
In soul and body clean.
With Israel's myriads sealed
Let all the nations meet
And show Thy mystery fulfilled,
The family complete.

Thomas Kelly: Zion's King Shall Reign Victorious (1806)

Zion's King shall reign victorious,
All the earth shall own His sway;
He will make His kingdom glorious,
He will reign through endless day.

Refrain
Mighty King, Thine arm revealing,
Now Thy glorious cause maintain,
Bring the nations help and healing,
Make them subject to Thy reign.

Nations now from God estrangèd,
Then shall see a glorious light,
Night to day shall then be changèd,
Heaven shall triumph in the sight.

Refrain

Then shall Israel, long dispersèd,
Mourning seek the Lord their God,
Look on Him Whom once they piercèd,
Own and kiss the chastening rod.

Refrain

The Saviour's face the ransomed nations bow;
O'erwhelmed at His almighty grace, forever new:
He shows His prints of love—they kindle to a flame!
And sound thro' all the worlds above the slaughtered Lamb.

Wake, Harp of Zion, Wake again

Wake, harp of Zion, wake again,
Upon thine ancient hill,
On Jordan's long deserted plain,
By Kedron's lowly rill.

The hymn shall yet in Zion swell,
That sounds Messiah's praise,
And thy loved Name, Emmanuel,
As once in ancient days.

For Israel yet shall own her King,
For her salvation waits,
And hill and dale shall sweetly sing,
With praise in all her gates.

O hasten, Lord, these promised days,
When Israel shall rejoice,
And Jew and Gentile join in praise,
With one united voice!

The whole triumphant host give thanks to God on high;
"Hail, Father, Son, and Holy Ghost," they ever cry.
Hail, Abraham's God, and mine! (I join the heav'nly lays,)
All might and majesty are Thine, and endless praise.